WOMAN LIBERATED

By Lois Gunden Clemens

HERALD PRESS, SCOTTDALE, PENNSYLVANIA

WOMAN LIBERATED
Copyright © 1971 by Herald Press, Scottdale, Pa. 15683
Library of Congress Catalog Care Number: 79-141830
International Standard Book Number: 0-8361-1634-8
Printed in the United States

Designed by Tom Hershberger

To my husband, Ernest,
Whose encouragement, cooperation, and support
Have enabled me to accept
An expanding ministry in community and church life,
This book is affectionately dedicated.

The Conrad Grebel Lectures

The Conrad Grebel Lectureship was set up in 1950 for the purpose of making possible an annual study by a Mennonite scholar of some topic of interest and value to the Mennonite Church and to other Christian people. It is administered by the Conrad Grebel Lectureship Committee appointed by and responsible to the Mennonite Board of Education. The committee appoints the lecturers, approves their subjects, counsels them during their studies, and arranges for the delivery of the lectures at one or more places.

The lectureship is financed by donors who contribute annually $500 each.

Conrad Grebel was an influential leader in the sixteenth-century Swiss Anabaptist movement and is honored as one of the founders of the Mennonite Church.

The lectures are published by Herald Press, Scottdale, Pa. 15683, as soon as feasible after the delivery of the lectures. The date of publication by Herald Press is indicated by parenthesis.

Lectures thus far delivered are as follows:

1952 -- Foundations of Christian Education, by Paul Mininger.

1953 -- The Challenge of Christian Stewardship (1955), by Milo Kauffman.

1954 -- The Way of the Cross in Human Relations (1958), by Guy F. Hershberger.

1955 -- The Alpha and the Omega (1955), by Paul Erb.

1956 -- The Nurture and Evangelism of Children (1959), by Gideon G. Yoder.

1957 -- The Holy Spirit and the Holy Life (1959), by Chester K. Lehman.

1959 -- The Church Apostolic (1960), by J. D. Graber.

1960 –– These Are My People (1962), by Harold S. Bender.
1963 –– Servant of God's Servants (1964), by Paul M. Miller.
1964 –– The Resurrected Life (1965), by John R. Mumaw.
1965 –– Creating Christian Personality (1966), by A. Don Augsburger.
1966 –– God's Word Written (1966), by J. C. Wenger.
1967 –– The Christian and Revolution (1968), by Melvin Gingerich.
1968-1969 –– The Discerning Community –– Church Renewal, by J. Lawrence Burkholder.
1970 –– Woman Liberated (1971), by Lois Gunden Clemens.

Introduction

This book is the thirteenth published title in the series of Conrad Grebel Lectures. This lectureship was established to enable an appointed scholar to spend a substantial block of time in study and reflection on a problem of vital concern to the church. He then shares the results of his study in a series of five lectures.

Lois Gunden Clemens' lectures on woman's relationships in her world offer unusual promise of personal and community enrichment. Too long have we overused half of our members (the men) and have scarcely used the other half (the women). Lois Clemens clearly points out the theological inadequacies of this practice; she also offers creative suggestions for ways in which the unique talents of women may be most effectively used.

This is not a "women's manifesto" to men: "you do this -- or else." This book has been written to both women and men. Each needs to study its message carefully and prayerfully. There is a note of sorrow for past failures, but there is not in this book a trace of bitterness or self-pity. Lois Clemens loves life, mankind, and the church. In this book she points the way to a more effective utilization and mobilization of the total human resources.

The fourteen previous Conrad Grebel lectures have all been men. Typical of many of the other committees and boards of the church, the Conrad Grebel Lectureship Committee is composed entirely of men. Perhaps it is also symbolic that when the first woman lecturer was chosen, she was asked to speak on a subject of interest to women. But it should be observed that during the time the committee was conducting negotiations with Lois Clemens for her series of lectures on the role of women, it was also conducting discussions with another woman for a series of lectures on the subject of Christian worship.

Women have served well and in large numbers for many years on the faculties of Mennonite schools and colleges. They have had highly significant assignments in foreign missions and relief work. They have been song leaders and are frequently the very backbone of the Christian education programs of the local congregations. In myriads of ways they are the service arm of the local congregation in its ministry to people in need. They have been writers and editors of our church publications. But their service on church boards is of much more recent origin and quantitatively much less significant, There have been women on the Mennonite Board of Education since since 1949 and on the Goshen College Board of Overseers since its inception in 1960. But only this year have women been appointed to two of the major administrative committees of the Mission Board -- the Health and Welfare Committee and the Overseas Committee. Perhaps we have come a long way, but we still have a long way to go.

June 23, 1970

Carl Kreider
Executive Secretary
Conrad Grebel Lectureship Committee

Foreword

It has been most meaningful for me to prepare the lectures that are the basis for this book. The experience has given me exciting insights into the way God's people are meant to function together.

I see the possibility of a new freedom of fellowship between men and women who together have found personhood in Christ. When individuals experience the reality of becoming new persons in Christ, they simply must communicate this exciting news to others. This impetus enables men and women to work side by side in the church without being conscious of whether they are male or female.

In attempting to clarify woman's role, I have sought to discover from all the available evidence how God views woman. Unfortunately it is difficult for the researcher to find in biblical studies much information about the women mentioned in the Scriptures. Often the scanty details concerning their ministry must be interpreted in the light of information about their historical settings. But the record is clear; God is no respecter of persons even in the matter of sex.

This presentation of woman is not in any way meant to place woman in opposition to man. Neither is it an attempt to take anything away from man. It aims rather to help woman achieve her God-ordained partnership with man in the work of the church. Women, if given the opportunity to develop and use their capabilities in the functioning life of the church, can add a significant dimension to it.

With men and women joining together to fulfill the purpose of the church in the world, congregational life might become a more vital expression of that purpose. It is my hope that God may use this study to create the vision needed to transform patterns of church life into the kind of sharing fellowship that characterized the early church.

Lois Gunden Clemens, Lansdale, Pennsylvania
June 1970

Contents

In the New Testament Era
In the Early Church
In the Missionary Movement
The Present Situation

The Nature of the Body of Christ
The Functioning of the Body
Principles of Biblical Interpretation
The Problematic Scripture Passages
Living Responsibility as Members

1
Who Is Woman?

The biblical view of woman must be the basis for any theology setting forth woman's relationship to God and her position in His kingdom. God's view of woman cannot be separated from His stated purposes in the creation of mankind in two parts -- male and female.

Both the nature and the implications of this duality must be recognized in order to understand the personal and social consequences inherent in the relatedness of its two component parts. Woman must be seen as an integral dimension of God's image reflected in mankind.

God's View of Woman

The Genesis account of what happened "in the beginning" states: "So God created man in his own image . . . male and female created he them." Here is enunciated the dual nature of mankind made in God's own image. A "she" exists alongside a "he" in created man; neither one alone embodies the totality of created man.

God had a definite purpose in making generic man a twofold being. He placed the woman alongside the

man because He saw that it was not good to have
one human being exist in solitude: it was not good
for man to be alone. For this reason God formed another human being suitable to be of help to man.
This helper was called the *woman,* which means the
she-man.

The word here used for "help" indicates more than
that of simply doing man's work or looking after his
physical needs. This word, also translated "helper," is
most commonly used in the Old Testament when referring to God as a help.[1] Built into man's nature is
his dependency upon God for a sustaining relationship
that both develops his personhood and gives it meaning and purpose. Over and over the Old Testament
shows God bringing this kind of help to man. Likewise woman brings to man a human relationship
through which he becomes a more complete person.
No other living creature could provide such com-
panionship for him; there had to be one who was
like himself and yet distinct from him.

This implies that man and woman were not meant
to be two independent, self-subsistent individuals having no need of each other. Rather, they are made to
be one dual being in a totality consisting of two distinct persons, one male and the other female. Each
one is a correlated component naturally oriented toward the other.[2] Such bipolarity of generic man is
not without purpose in its specific design.

In the first place, this polarity is the basis for com-

plementarity between the two sexes. In being created male and female, man and woman are meant
to complete each other. Their unity is not limited to
the "one-flesh" union for the procreative function of
the family. In the totality of their living, male and
female complete each other through uniting their
separate corresponding elements.

The incompleteness of each sex which reaches beyond the biological sphere calls for union and communion in many areas. Just as both male and female
are necessary for the creation and continuation of
human life, so this fundamental pattern of cooperation
should be characteristic of all human interrelationships.[3] Women and men were made to complete each
other mentally, spiritually, and emotionally, as well as
biologically.

Because of the dual nature of the human being, the
challenge of the complementary element arouses what
is most noble and profound in man or woman. Without woman, man cannot reach the most complete
development of his manhood. In like manner, woman
needs to relate to man in order to attain the most
profound level of her femininity.[4]

Second, in the polarity of the two sexes, the Creator has planted an element of creative tension. As a
perpetual impetus to the search for joy in uniting the
complementary parts, this tension urges men and
women on to praiseworthy achievements.

It is a unique tension, both in quality and effect,

as a result of its complementary differentiation. It can generate many kinds of creativity in various spheres of activity. This is apparent, for example, in the awakening of dormant personal characteristics or potentialities, in effectual cooperation for achieving common goals, or in the blending of various insights needed to solve our human problems.[5]

Third, the polarity of male and female provides the basis for establishing relationships with others. God uses the natural orientation of one sex toward the other to draw a person out of his loneliness, driving him to seek a relationship with another person.[6]

Creating the two sexes was God's declaration of the fact that it is not good for either man or woman to be alone. Sex is not merely part of nature for the propagation of the human race. It is related to God's purposes for man's happiness and usefulness. The more each sex can act in unconscious self-possession, the taller it causes the other one to stand. Herein are to be seen the dimensions of dignity and meaning that God gave to sex.

Since man and woman exist for each other, the need for fulfilling this partnership is built into all men and women. The establishment of partner relationships is the obligation of all; it does not apply simply to marriage. The opportunities and necessities of our life together involve the sexes in many kinds of associations other than the central form of partnership in marriage.

Such associations provide possibilities enabling the woman and the man to function together for constructive ends. Created with reference to each other, male and female are bound together in a mutual dependence in all the activities and concerns of human life. No human activity is completely independent of the man-woman relationship. True partnership includes the cross-fertilization of mind and spirit so necessary for a creative approach to life.[7] With harmonious cooperation between the sexes, each can help the other to realize his best potential. Without it, there is an imbalance of the forces necessary for releasing the springs of manhood and womanhood.

Man and woman are fulfilling a high purpose of their sexual polarity when they are helping each other to realize the best that is within them. Such a mutually enlarging and creative relationship should be characteristic of all the relationships between man and woman.[8] This should be particularly true within the fellowship of the church.

Whether the Christian is married or single, he cannot forget the profound truth stated in 1 Corinthians 11:11 that neither is the man without the woman, nor the woman without the man, in the Lord. In their relationships in the church, then, all men and women -- both the married and the unmarried -- need to experience free encounter with one another. Those called to the single life and those called to marriage are under the same obligation to live in belongingness, one sex with the other, in the unity of the body of Christ.[9]

One of the consequences of generic man's sexual duality is the importance of constructive male-female relationships. For these relationships to be of benefit both to the individual and to society, they must begin on the basis of personhood, rather than on that of sex category. This approach unlocks the relationship from a strictly sexual focus and thereby releases a broader creative potential. The result is a better fulfillment of God's intent in the dual-being design He chose for mankind.

When God's primary purpose in creating the two sexes is seen as that of setting up meaningful personal relationships rather than producing children, then sexuality can be viewed as something beyond the body-aspect of life. It can be understood as belonging to God's scheme of things for the good of all. It must never be regarded as simply the means of satisfying a biological function. Since physical sex is only part of the whole man or woman, no man or woman should be viewed only -- or even primarily -- as a sex object.

A wrong view of God's purpose for placing man and woman together can lead to false values and expectations regarding male-female relationships. If physical sex is considered as the primary reason for the existence of man and woman, this puts a false label on their relationship experiences. Such a label suggests physical relationships as the surest and shortest way to fulfillment. Acceptance of this false idea can lead only to disillusion, even within marriage.

Society's present obsession with physical sex is a mockery of God's act of placing woman alongside man so that the two might enhance and complete each other's lives through a mutually beneficial relationship. The church should be clearly showing this in a positive manner. At stake is the quality of life experienced together as members of the body of Christ. Right attitudes about man-woman encounters experienced in this setting could add helpful dimensions to patterns of relationship in the marriage setting. The quality of all interpersonal living could be improved through better understanding of the kind of help God meant woman to be to man.

The family should be the primary social group in which each member, whether child or adult, learns through personal experience the necessity of human interdependence. Such experience reveals the way in which relating to one another brings into fruition the latent potentialities of each person's being. It is an important function of the Christian family to help each member develop the powers with which God has endowed him.[10]

Recognizing the importance of the relationship factor in the polarity of the two sexes is essential for understanding the biblical symbol of the church as the bride of Christ. Marriage represents the most com-

plete personal commitment possible between a man
and a woman. It unites the two into a living, growing relationship designed to develop fuller personhood.
In like manner the church is a body of persons completely committed to Christ in a living, growing relationship. This relationship is the way by which the
Christian may reach the highest fulfillment of his
being.

God's view of woman, then, sees her as an essential
part of generic man made in His likeness. Due to the
differentiation in the male and the female elements
of total man, each part needs to be completed by relating to the other. Man and woman are interdepen-
dent. The two parts must function together if they
are to represent God's total image in generic man.
Relationships are therefore basic to God's purposes
in bisexuality. God looked upon His creation of man
and woman as a fitting culmination to His creative
activity, pronouncing it to be very good. And according to His design, woman is to share with man the
dignity of bearing God's image and carrying out His
purposes for mankind.

Man's View of Woman

Anthropologists familiar with life in societies around
the world report a variety of attitudes and judgments
about women in primitive societies. Traditionally
these societies have developed a myth of feminine
evil.

This sort of attitude stems from the primitive male's inability to identify with woman because she is different from him. Unable to unravel the mystery of her belonging to a separate category, he tends to think of her as having some supernatural power of evil over him. Preliterate cultures exhibit a worldwide fear of woman's sexual functions. These fears are usually formalized in various sanctions and restrictions that give her something less than full-fledged membership in the tribe.[11]

The primitive male readily projects such fears into antagonisms and derogatory attitudes. He may insist that women are not only evil, but inferior and unimportant as well.

The myth of feminine inferiority has become a more widespread belief. In most human cultures woman is considered a lower human being than the male, less wise and less intelligent than he, and lacking in many of his capacities and abilities. It is evident that when woman must be the cricket on the hearth caring for the young while man is the eagle on the wing broadening his experience and increasing his observations, her limited experience makes her appear less highly endowed than man.[12]

The male, by insisting that woman is inferior and valueless, can find a way to deal with the fears and antagonisms growing out of his inability to comprehend her differences. He can insist that she should be given a restricted role or can assign to her some role

which removes her from the sphere of competition.[13]
In primitive societies such segregation of woman in
the religious practices of the tribe allows man to keep
religion largely in his own hands. This gives a greater degree of credibility and reverence to his powers
as the dominant male.

It is easy for cultural attitudes based on differences
eventually to regard these differences as deficiencies.
Patriarchal societies have tended to utilize male and
female differences as a reason for considering man as
being superior and woman as inferior. Here the
example of the historical British attitude toward a ruling monarch might be an interesting commentary.
When a ruling succession places a queen on the
throne, there is no problem in accepting her superiority as a ruler. Yet how many Englishmen would
consider electing a queen if that were the necessary
process?

The status of women has fluctuated greatly throughout history. Differing attitudes characteristic of certain
periods and cultures have been documented.

In the history of God's people, the record shows
woman's position as something less than that original-
ly ordained by God. Even then she was a noble and
exalted figure by contrast with her counterpart in the
surrounding pagan cultures. But her status was continually lowered as time moved toward the coming of
Christ. Largely through the influence of heathen cults,
the Jewish woman's freedom among men became

more and more circumscribed. The narrow spirit of the religious leaders of Jesus' day ascribed little value to woman. She was regarded more as man's chattel than as a person in her own right. The rabbis allowed her no instruction in the law; lacking this, she had no place in God's service. She was considered to be morally inferior to man, and had no more right than a Gentile to join in the after-meal grace.[14]

Christ brought release to woman from her agelong debasement. In His kingdom she is not to be regarded as the object of man's domination and desire, which was the pagan concept. Instead Jesus created the image of her own personal worth.

In the early church and during the first four centuries of the Christian period in Rome, woman was held in high esteem. Her position was secure, giving her both power and dignity for her time. All this was lost when the barbarian invasions from the north again brought the pagan view of woman to bear upon her status.[15]

In the ensuing centuries the church fathers spoke of women in quite contemptuous terms. Some of the deficiencies ascribed to them were attributable to the restrictions placed upon their educational development together with their exclusion from social life. They were to be avoided as dangerous temptresses waiting to beguile man, according to some of the church fathers.[16] By the time of the middle ages women were rejected still more drastically than in preceding periods. The witchcraft concept of quite recent periods developed out of this setting. Even today many men think of woman largely in terms of a dehumanized sex object or a status symbol.

And so society has been conditioned to believe that women are something less than men. They are considered to be human beings, but beings of a lower sort, having less wisdom and intelligence than the male, and lacking in most of his endowed abilities and capacities. In most parts of the world women have traditionally not had equal opportunities with men to develop their capacities and to become persons of worth in their own right. They have been prejudged as a class rather than fairly judged as persons.

These myths about women which have been accepted as truth throughout history have been disproved by the findings of modern science. It can be shown that most of what has been said to their discredit is false and that in certain ways women are better endowed than men. These relevant and available facts are not widely recognized or discussed. But man can no longer permit himself to accept his long-held belief in woman's inferiority. Accepting the truth in this matter will free men along with women, for without the full development of woman, no man can be his best self.[17]

Christ's View of Woman

The Creation story states that woman, along with

man, was made in the image of God. Various Old
Testament references to be considered in a later
chapter indicate that even in those times she had a
real part in the religious life of God's people. In the
period between the Old and the New Testaments,
women's religious privileges were circumscribed as a
result of Israel's closer ties with surrounding heathen
nations.

Such was the situation into which Jesus introduced
a different view. He treated women as persons with
whom He could relate meaningfully. He practiced
the principle of equality for both sexes in spiritual
matters and privileges. It is to His attitudes, teachings, and principles that the church must look for
direction and authority on the role of woman in its
life and service.[18]

What Jesus introduced concerning woman appeared
to be something new. It was, however, really something which had been gradually lost by Israel. Here
was another of the areas in which Jesus was fulfilling
the law by teaching a more complete understanding of
it. He opened to woman the love and respect that
reached beyond the sexual and also gave her full
human value outside of marriage.[19]

While Judaism excluded woman from the study of
the Torah, Christ opened to women and men alike
the way to the knowledge of God. His call to salvation recorded in Matthew 11:28-30 was for all who
were weary and heavily burdened. This certainly was

a welcome invitation to the women of His day. In
placing personal salvation within the sphere of the
individual, He showed no distinction between man
and woman. He spoke of new life to the Samaritan
woman at the well just as He did to Nicodemus. And
He commended Mary of Bethany for sitting at His
feet to hear His word, an act unheard of for a
woman in that time.

Jesus' words, whether of command or of promise,
were always the same for women as for men. He saw
woman as being created by God for the same end as
man. What was sin for one was also sin for the other.
Both alike were commanded to be perfect as God is
perfect. Does this not mean that Christ was placing
woman's human personality on the very same level
as that of man? As moral beings responsible to God,
man and woman are not subordinated in any manner.
Jesus saw woman's worth as residing in her own person, rather than in her relation to man.[20]

Christ's view of woman is summarized by Paul in
Galatians 3:28. In Christ, he says, there is neither
male nor female, just as there is neither Jew nor
Greek, bond nor free, because all are one in Christ.
In other words, in Christ the distinctions between
male and female have no meaning: God's relationship
to redeemed mankind disregards all differences. Even
in the matter of sex, God is no respecter of persons.

In Christian relationships such distinctions as sex
no longer count since anyone who is in Christ is a

new creation. The one who was a Jew is now a Christian. He who was a Gentile is now a Christian. He who was a male is now a Christian. Likewise she who was a female is now a Christian. Out of many human differences, each new creation in Christ emerges as a Christian. All are one by virtue of being a new kind of person in God's likeness, according to Ephesians 4:24. In this new creation all human differences lose any essential significance.[21]

To Jesus the matter of woman's status in His kingdom was a religious question. It mattered little to Him what standards society had set up to govern human relationships. Matthew 22:16. In the kingdom of heaven all human barriers were to be broken down. It is a continuing duty of His church to express the reality of a community without dividing lines.[22] Mundane distinction, such as male and female, will not be the standard determining relationships in a body where "Christ is all, and in all" (Colossians 3:11).

Jesus' reverence for the worth of the individual person caused Him to consider unacceptable any system which acted in disregard of the person. For this reason He often clashed with the religious power structures of His day. In many such instances He came to the rescue of women. He showed His own high evaluation of woman's personhood in His attitude toward the woman taken in adultery, for example, or the woman who anointed His feet with oil, or the one healed on the Sabbath, or the Samaritan woman. He was never lacking in respect for any woman, even the most wretched of them. Always He showed a sensitivity of feeling which never violated any individual's personhood.

With His coming, therefore, a new day dawned for woman, granting her the right to become the person God meant her to be. He saw her first as a human personality, and second as a woman. This was in contrast to the Jewish and pagan views which saw her primarily as a sexual entity and gave no consideration to her personhood.[23]

Jesus' recognition that woman is above all a person is His declaration of her rights to self-realization and fulfillment. She is to be thought of as an individual rather than to be categorized simply as a woman. Women have individual abilities and needs which vary to the same extent as do those of men; they should be given the same opportunity to discover and respond to the unique aspects of their beings.[24] Only in this way can they become the persons God designed them to be. Many women have lacked this opportunity. They have been restricted by the traditional view of those around them, as well as by their own narrow vision of themselves and their God-given role in His purposes for them.

Selfhood can be realized only by the process of endlessly being drawn out of itself into larger ends.[25] Belonging to the family of God and participating in its life provides such ends. By being admitted into fellowship with God, the believer finds a reason for living and a reality that gives him a sense of worth and supports him in his weakness. In fellowship with other members of God's family, he is drawn out of the prison of his self-concern into larger kingdom concerns.

It was just such fulfillment of self that Jesus opened to woman in offering her all the rights and privileges of membership in His kingdom. As she participates fully in the life of the community of believers, she finds that more and more of her potentialities are being realized. Her selfhood develops through this experience of finding its center beyond itself and in relation to others. She comes to know and accept herself more realistically through these relationships. She becomes more self-confident and more mature as she learns to face facts not only outside but also within herself. This in turn gives her the self-reliance that makes for the best possible use of her capabilities.[26]

And so Jesus reiterated God's original statement of woman's intrinsic worth as a person. She contains within herself the purpose of her existence. She, like man, is a human individual whose value and rights must be recognized.[27] This fact is important not only for establishing satisfactory male-female relationships in all areas of life, but also for understanding her role in the church.

The Church's View of Woman

The heart of Christian theology lies in the concept of relationship. Theology is relevant when it shows who a person is in relation to a living God, giving insights into the nature and destiny of man. It indicates the worth each person has from God's viewpoint. The church should be providing such a sense of identity to those seeking to know the meaning of their existence.

The biblical account teaches that woman was created in the image of God. She is the female part of a dual personality made in two separate beings. She is meant to function together with man in a complementary relationship mutually beneficial to both of them. God's purposes for created man are for her as well as for the male. She is destined to relate to her Creator and carry out His purposes for her.

This is the biblical view of woman that the church should be giving to those women wanting to know who they are and what life is all about. It explains the necessity and the importance of male-female cooperation in accomplishing God's purposes. It means that in the life of the church men and women will function together as a body.

Attitudes of the church about woman and her worth in God's kingdom are reflected in the degree to which she may participate in the functioning life of the community of believers. Women should be given the same opportunity as men to contribute fully to that life according to their individual gifts. In this way the church can help women function with purpose in the areas where they are best prepared to serve.

Just as the cooperation of both man and woman is necessary in the family for representing the totality of God's image, so should it be in the church. There should be women participating fully with men on issues that affect the total body, for they could bring important insights and understandings to decision-making.

Present patterns of church organization and life, however, reflect very little acceptance of woman as man's equal in the body of Christ. Church planning and policy-making have long been a men's monopoly. In order to have any part in decision-making or programming or policy-making, women have had to do so in their own women's organizations apart from the regular church organization. This kind of segregation hardly reflects a literal interpretation of the teaching that in Christ there is no distinction between male and female.

It is unfortunate that the church has not been ready to face the implications of Christ's ethic concerning woman in relation to man as expressed in His attitudes and teachings. This ethic is at times more clearly visible in social and cultural changes attributable to its influence on Western culture than in theology and ecclesiastical practice.[28] If in Christ there is no such thing as male or female, why should the intelligence and insight of capable women be ignored at all levels of the church organization?

Since Christ calls woman to grow up into the full stature of her personhood in Him, the church should see that she is given every opportunity for such growth in all possible ways. Only thus can she develop according to the pattern of her particular strengths and abilities. The more fully she can do this, the more authentic will be her witness.

In the church community a woman ought never be labeled first according to her sex. She should rather be thought of as a person offering the possibility of creative relationships in a nonfamily setting. This was clearly the approach of Jesus in relating to women. It is an approach to man-woman relationships that could provide a more secure position for the single and the widowed women in the church body. Built on integrity combined with complete freedom, such relationships could be most constructive.

Among the Anabaptists the man-woman relationship was enhanced because of their common loyalty to a religious faith. Their life centered upon common endeavors in the work of the Lord, even in the marriage setting. Every member of the Anabaptist community, whether man or woman, was considered a missionary. Here was equality of the sexes in the life of the church. Putting God first enabled these men and women to work side by side in the church without consciousness of differences in sex.[29]

The church today might find this kind of approach helpful in thinking about women's role in its total life and witness. This would mean concentrating on the common endeavors laid upon men and women alike because of their common allegiance to Christ. The impetus of sharing the exciting news about the reality of becoming new persons in Christ might still be the best way of enabling men and women to work side by side without too much attention to differences in sex.

A similar picture of the early church at work is recorded in Acts and in the letters of the New Testament. Here we read what actually happened when men and women began to "believe in the Lord Jesus Christ." In outlook and pattern of life these people were pioneers of a new way of life. This transformation of their living came as by faith in Jesus they grasped the new order He represented. They saw that this new order had to be expressed in human relationships.[30] And this meant full participation by all, as each believer gave highest priority to expressing outwardly and effectively his inward spiritual certainty. Both men and women eagerly joined in the witness to this certainty according to their personal abilities and perceptions.

The church's view of who woman is should be identical with the biblical view expressed in the

Creation account and in the gospel record of Christ's attitude toward woman. Jesus revealed God's original intent for her in extending to her first-class citizenship in God's kingdom. It is only when the church has been influenced by cultural and social patterns that woman is denied her status of full citizenship in the church.

It is time for the Christian community to consider seriously the view of woman that is reflected in its functioning life. If the church as a body is to represent the reality of the new creation in Christ, the implications of Galatians 3:28 dare not be disregarded.

2
The Problem of Roles

The problem of woman's role is man's problem as well as woman's, since role is fundamentally a matter of relationship. By God's design woman is destined to function together with man in creative relationships. Right male-female relationships are basic to a true understanding of the role of either sex. Woman's understanding of her role cannot be separated from man's about his; the two are closely interrelated.

The relationship between men and women in the church regulates woman's status and role in its life and witness. In the history of the church this relationship has never been entirely fixed. Always there is a tension between what comes to a church from the gospel and what is due to other influences. Much comes to a church from its own past history and tradition as well as from the society of which it is a part. In society the position of woman has varied greatly in different times and places; it undergoes change as new circumstances affect society's attitudes.[1]

Man's Delineation of Roles

Deep and complex psychological conditions are involved in men's attitudes about how women are to function in society. It is more difficult for a man to identify his masculinity than for a woman to establish her femininity. Hence he has a greater problem in clarifying his role than does woman. In a male-dominated society, he has tended to assign woman's role to her by reference to what he conceives his to be.

A girl early becomes aware that she will grow up to be a woman like her mother. Through the maturing of her body she achieves womanhood; she realizes her femininity by becoming capable of attaining motherhood. For a boy, by contrast, growing up to be a man is not simply a natural process of bodily maturation. There are certain standards for him to meet before he will be judged as having attained manhood. He must prove himself to be a man by acquiring some trait or skill or by passing some test of achievement. In many societies he must undergo a special initiation ceremony by which his manhood is established.[2]

The traditional view of masculinity calls for an endless process of achieving in which the male must continuously prove himself to be a man. Therefore the man's sense of his masculinity is characterized throughout by uncertainty and the challenge of objective achievement.[3]

The anthropologist Margaret Mead sees this as the reason for the male's need for a prestige greater than that accorded to woman. His need for such prestige can be recognized in every known society, she says. Whatever activities a society considers appropriate for men are rated by that society as its most important functions. Often men's sureness of their manhood is associated with their right or ability to do something from which women are excluded.[4] Consequently the male tends to feel that he establishes his masculine identity by being superior to woman.

Because woman's identity is more closely bound to nature than is man's, she can act more unconsciously as a person, without reference to her sex, than a man. Thinking of themselves as individuals, women are often surprised to learn that men who are interacting with them are very aware of their sex. Although under certain circumstances they can forget that they are women, men seem unable to do so.[5]

The roles expressing masculinity and femininity are not the same in the various cultures around the world. All societies have differentiation of roles, but what is considered feminine activity in one may be regarded as masculine in another. Such interchange of roles indicates that some roles are neither masculine nor feminine. Hence the traditional activities assigned to either sex in a given culture may not necessarily be related in any direct way to sex differentiation. In North America men are taught to think that women are supposed to express emotion. In South America men may express their feelings openly.

Man today is caught in a tradition regarding roles
that was passed on to him as part of his social
heritage. He has attributed this social tradition to the
biological order of things. Although he is now discovering that some of his traditional beliefs about
women are false, he does not readily change his long-
held views. Some of these same attitudes of society
have also influenced the church's thinking about
woman's place in its mission.

Present Confusion About Roles

American women need understanding as they attempt to find their place in society. They have been
more or less stereotyped according to the pattern
preferred by men, and this pattern rates them as
having less potentiality than the male. Consequently
many women have not been allowed to develop their
own individual life patterns. They have filled their
stereotyped roles, serving the male's misconceived
needs for himself in relationships between the sexes.
In the process, both men and women have become
confused about their roles.[6] They have equated
traditionally assigned roles with masculinity and
femininity.

Self-made man has tended to think of woman as
his equal only insofar as she could equal the model
of his self-made image. Many women have consequently felt forced to prove their equality by competing with men on their own ground, trying to

show as it were that they too could be "men." This has, in effect, kept womankind within her traditional place in man's frame of reference. The result has been that granting women equal rights has not led to giving them equal roles in the expression of their particular concerns. With little opportunity to participate in decision-making, their concerns are inadequately represented in the councils of men today.[7]

Both men and women should be helped to see that woman makes her greatest contribution, not by trying to compete with men as if she were man, but rather on the basis of herself as an individual person. Men must cease to think of her as belonging to a secondary sex. Such categorizing immediately assigns to her a second-class status that makes impossible any concept of equality with man. Men must learn to accept women as equals who, like themselves, may differ greatly in abilities and interests.[8] In that case, men and women could function together more creatively and constructively to their mutual benefit. The fact of male-female complementarity would add significance to their cooperative efforts. It would mean bringing into focus a more complete human view of things by adding woman's particular perspective to man's.

Cultural Change and Role Problems

Changing cultural patterns cause discontent and

confusion about the respective roles of men and women within the new patterns. The traditional life-style becomes modified so that there is no longer a prescribed place for each individual. Both men and women experience psychological problems in times of rapid historical change, but men usually feel more threatened than women.[9] Men are apt to lose some of their time-honored status in the process, while women are more apt to gain something from it.

In recent centuries the roles and functions of women have undergone considerable modification. The change began when the Industrial Revolution moved manufacturing from the home to the factory. This revolutionized the way of life in the home. Many of woman's earlier chores were now done by machine outside the home. Where men and women had largely worked together on the land and in the home, men have been removed from the family setting during a long working day.

A few generations ago family tasks were frequently shared by members of two or more generations living under the same roof or located nearby. Now the mother is usually the only adult present in the home to assume responsibility throughout most of the day. Furthermore, the family is more likely to be found among strangers in a suburban or urban setting.[10]

Woman's life-span has been extended and at the same time her years of childbearing shortened. As

early as in her late thirties she may find herself
free to engage in activities outside the home, part
time at first and eventually full time. This gives her
a freedom unique to twentieth-century woman. In
the new patterns of family living she may feel that
in the home she is left out of her traditional role of
influence in society. Often she is an educated woman
prepared to make a significant contribution to life
in the larger world. The cultural change brought by
increasing education for women has thus been
another factor adding to confusion about woman's
role.

Educated women today face difficulties as they seek
to know their rightful place in society. Although they
are more free to choose where to direct their energies, they face conflicting values, needs, and circumstances. For most of them marriage comes first, but
they want very much to be both women and full
human beings. They feel that they should contribute
beyond the wifehood and motherhood spheres they
are happy to accept. Therefore they hope to find
ways of participating in life outside the home in ways
that do not imperil their roles as wives and mothers.[11]

Such women, if they confine themselves exclusively
to home activities, may begin to feel that many of
their developed capacities are going to waste. They
want to be able to apply their minds to some useful
ends. Having experienced the challenge of working
creatively as fully trained and responsible persons,

they often find that homemaking uses only a part of their potentialities and energies. So they want to commit themselves to additional tasks that will draw upon the larger range of their talents and thinking.[12]

How fortunate it would be if these women found it possible to devote themselves to such tasks within the life of the church when they are fully prepared to do so. Many persons in the church, however, cannot understand why a Christian woman with a family should be interested in anything beyond her home. They believe that a woman could have no more important or fulfilling work in the church or in society than to bear and nurture children. It is true that some mothers would not care to spend their time on extensive activities outside the home, particularly during their busiest periods of child-rearing. But for others, some creative use of their powers in the broader sphere might heighten their contributions in the family sphere. A mother's horizons in some way must be expanded to provide the help and stimulation needed by the family members as they develop. It must also be recognized that as the mainstream of life continues to bypass the home, a mother may feel that she must be responsibly involved in that life outside, where decisions are being made that will affect the life of her family.[13]

Never before in the history of any known society has woman tried to occupy her full time with motherhood. In past eras women served as productive partners with their husbands in farm or craft teams. Children shared in the household work and largely organized their own play. With the world continually entering their homes, their days were peopled with many adults in addition to the extended family members living under the same roof.[14] The altering of such circumstances has influenced the changing ideal for womanhood.

In a changing society, woman's role cannot be determined in the light of what it was in the past when she had to live within the particular sphere assigned to her in a different social setting. Change has disrupted many old patterns that formerly fixed woman's prescribed place. Twentieth-century changes have been opening to woman new opportunities to develop more of her unrealized resources. This has been much more true of her life outside the church than within it, where her developed resources have for the most part not been utilized.

Whether a woman adds outside dimensions to her career in the home should be determined by her own personality and capacities and her own life-style. But significant involvement in the life of the church to the degree compatible with her other duties and obligations should be possible for any woman, even if she is a wife and mother.

The Matter of Headship

There is further confusion concerning woman's

role because of confusion about the meaning and
sphere of the headship mentioned by the Apostle
Paul in 1 Corinthians 11:2-16.

From the context of this passage, it would seem
that Paul is referring specifically to headship in the
husband-wife relationship. One of Paul's primary
concerns in this whole letter is for the preservation
of the marriage relationship. The behavior of some
married women in the church was troubling others in
the fellowship, and was also being misunderstood by
persons on the outside observing their worship
practices.

The language of these verses does not clearly
delineate whether the word *man* is used in the
restricted sense of *husband* or with the broader
meaning of man in general. The same is true of the
word *woman*, which can have either the restricted
meaning of *wife* or the more general one. Hence
theologians differ in applying the principle of headship. Some believe that it is only in reference to the
husband-wife relationship. Others would apply it to
the larger sphere of man-woman relationships.

Some English translations other than the King
James Version, such as Today's English Version,
use the words *husband* and *wife* in the key verses
referring to the specific relationship involved. Thus
in verse 3 the *husband* is said to be the head of
the *wife*. In verse 5 a woman is described as dishonoring her *husband* when she participates in the

worship service with her head uncovered. This is in keeping with the customary use of the veil in that culture to symbolize the marriage relationship; a married woman appearing unveiled in public disgraced her husband, not man in general.

Aside from its sphere of reference, the meaning of headship must be clarified. The designation of headship does not indicate superior status or understanding. It rather designates the responsibility for coordinating any action that involves more than one person. This kind of coordination is necessary for order and concerted action when the members of a committee function together, for example.

The nature of the headship of the husband over the wife is further explained in Ephesians 5. Here headship is described as the authority of self-sacrificing love exemplified in the way Christ loved the church. Headship must be understood in the light of verse 33, which states that every man must love his wife as himself and that every wife must respect her husband. If the husband loves his wife as he loves himself, he will certainly respect her as a full person in her own right and will regard her as a vital contributor to their life together. This kind of equal consideration of her would merit the fullest respect from the wife. Thus the husband and wife would be subject to each other, as all Christians are to be, having reverence one for the other. Neither one would lord it over the other, for each would give first consideration to the other. This is sexual equality.

In the middle of this passage explaining man's headship over woman as God's order in creation, Paul refers in verse 11 to another order, that of redemption. He says that as far as being in the Lord is concerned, both are equal. The man is not "in the Lord" in any different relationship than is woman. This is equivalent to the Galatians 3:28 statement that all are one in Christ.

Another reference to the idea of male-female equality in the Lord is found in 1 Corinthians 11:7. Here Paul says that woman is the glory of man, but not his image. This is in contrast to man's being both the image and glory of God, and in keeping with the Genesis 1:27 statement that woman shares with man the image of God, which is to say that she is no more remote from God than is man.[15] Headship does not mean that woman must relate to God through man. In God's kingdom woman's worth is not found in her relation to man. She is not the moon in the human cosmos having only such light as she reflects from the sun. In God's kingdom she is a planet of the same order as man.[16]

Headship then does not mean domination of the husband over the wife. The man has no right to consider that his wife exists only to serve him and make life pleasant for him. That would be assigning her a difference in rank from him rather than a difference in kind, which would be a return to the pre-Christian evaluation of woman.[17]

This headship passage does say something about the relationship between husband and wife as they function together as a team. The man has the responsibility of initiating and coordinating the cooperative effort which supports their life together. As partners they respect and reverence each other as equals, although different in kind. Their differences of masculinity and femininity give neither superiority nor inferiority to either one of the two; rather, these differences are complementary as each partner brings some special area of superiority to contribute to the other. Both are free to contribute to the partnership the best of their own personhood.

If the headship principle is to be applied to life in the church, it should not be different from the pattern established for the husband-wife relationship. It cannot mean the exclusion of woman from the discerning and deciding functions of the Christian community. It should mean that women would participate along with men in policy-making groups, such as church councils or general governing boards, according to their individual gifts and capabilities. This is not in any way usurping the authority of final responsibility residing in headship. The headship principle does not eliminate woman from the team; her partnership there is as necessary as it is in the husband-wife team.

Results of Superiority Attitudes

Throughout the centuries man has tended to think
that his masculinity is expressed by showing himself
superior to woman. This confusion about his masculine characteristics has led to some undesirable consequences in man-woman relationships.

As long as man feels superior to woman, the
problem of roles cannot be solved. Right man-woman
relationships are not possible without mutual respect and reverence for each other as persons. If
man thinks he must show himself superior to woman,
he feels he must dominate her. Whether man's domination results from disregarding or from overpowering
woman's point of view, it destroys the meaning of
their relationship. Human relationships can be
ennobling only when each person is allowed the
right of being fully himself and is considerate of how
others think and feel.[18]

Men who think of women as not being their
equals are impoverishing themselves as well as
women. Men are the losers when women have had
to live in a perpetual state of personal and intellectual impoverishment.

Society still tends to regard the wife as subordinate
to the dominant male. It is traditionally accepted that
on the marital level the male's interests are to be
served first; his talents must be developed as fully
as possible, while little concern is given to developing

the wife's potential. She is expected to find fulfillment through the achievements of her husband,
whom she has helped to attain success.[19]

Women who are not allowed to develop their
potential are robbed of their birthright. They are not
the only ones who lose in the process, however;
society has been deprived of valuable resources which
could have been of benefit to all. Furthermore, capable women prepared to make their contribution
may be prevented from doing so in a free and re-
laxed manner by men's attitudes toward them. Even
women who think deeply and have clear insights
may not have the courage to use their native intelligence in the presence of men who discount it.[20]

Conflicting ideas about woman's proper place add
distinct strains to the marriage relationship. When
the husband and wife do not agree about her rights,
duties, and privileges, the difficult process of marriage
adjustment is greatly complicated.

Because woman's role is generally viewed as
secondary to man's, it comes to be thought of as an
inferior role. This allows woman to be seen simply
as the extension of her husband instead of an individual person in her own right. Consequently a
man may think of his wife, along with his house or
his car, as an object contributing to his self-image.[21]
When a woman senses that she is something less than
a full person in her husband's thinking, she may
begin to spar with him for whatever advantage might

be open to her. This can only lead to a competitive struggle for getting the most out of the situation on the part of both. Such competition indicates that the true nature and purpose of male-female complementarity is neither understood nor practiced.

A wife's frustration over inadequate fulfillment may unconsciously result in aggressive behavior on her part, making her less lovable and more unhappy with herself. Her failure to achieve reality for herself can twist the lives of many children and men out of shape along with hers. This is a heavy toll to pay because of distorted man-woman relationships.

Marriage should be an interchange of experience that stimulates greater creative growth and development of both partners. Marriage must be built on mutual respect, which disallows any ideas of superiority or inferiority. Men would find their homelife happier if they could learn to help their wives become what they were destined to be. Here the church should be setting a better pattern. If the Christian fellowship could establish the image of woman as a person functioning in her own right, this could contribute to happier marriages.

The present obsession with sex is another consequence of the inferior position man has given to woman. When man relates to woman simply on the basis of her biological makeup and function, he brings corruptive influences into his relationship with her. Man assigns value to her according to her attractiveness as a sex symbol. Women respond to the behavior of males toward them. Men who place a high premium on sexual attractiveness cause women to concentrate on making themselves as appealing to men as they can.[22] This kind of undue emphasis has confused and perverted the true purpose of sex to degrading ends. It has resulted in making woman into an abstract commodity in the form of the Hollywood love goddess. With right attitudes toward woman's personhood, there could never have been the tragedy of Marilyn Monroe, who was absolutely denied the right to exist as a human being.

When man becomes the exploiter in a sex-caste system, he destroys himself along with his victim. In courtship, mutual manipulation to gain any possible advantage from the situation plays havoc with the integrity of male-female relationships. What kind of preparation for marriage is this? Furthermore, in the broader spheres of life this system can distort the male's sense of his own importance since it makes available to him a noncompetitive servant class to do his bidding. Men who get things done by ordering others to do them and who make decisions binding others to courses of action without involving them in the decision-making tend to think more highly of themselves than they ought to think. They manifest a certain arrogance of power, marked by a lack of humility, patience, and adaptability.[23]

Woman cannot find her rightful role until she is no longer given inferior-class standing. Sex differences meant to have a complementary function dare not mark one part of generic man as superior to the other; both parts alike were made in God's likeness. Since both men and women have a worthwhile contribution to make, both should have equal opportunity to contribute. For too long the male has, perhaps unconsciously, kept the management of affairs in his own hands to satisfy his need to feel superior; this has upset the God-ordained complementary cooperation of the two sexes. Women must now help men discover that complementing each other rather than competing with each other is the best way for both of them to find the true worth of their masculinity and femininity.

Complementarity of Roles

There is no society which does not recognize that there are differences between men and women. While many of these differences are developed as part of cultural patterns, some are actually biological differences stemming from sex differentiation. In comparing biological differences between men and women, what is under consideration is difference for a purpose. God created generic man in the dual form of male and female so that each might bring something unique to their interrelationship.

These differences are the very basis for enrichment of life as men and women function together side by side in partnership. They are at the root of male-female complementarity. Men and women were not designed to be identical. They were meant to be complementary in the sense of "to make complete" out of two mutually completing parts. This does not imply seeing eye to eye; a person is completed by what he does not have rather than by what he already has. Differences of viewpoint brought together result in a wider outlook. If man and woman are to live creatively in the state of belongingness for which they were made, they must adventure forth side by side in confidence and mutual trust, ready to learn what each can contribute to the other.

Women are to be seen not only as persons, but as persons not identical with the male. Difference in sex means difference in attitudes, viewpoints, and behavior. Equality of rights does not therefore indicate identity of being. In this sense, women make their best contribution to society through their special endowments as women rather than by trying to be identical with men.

Christ restored to woman's personhood its due importance, placing it on an equal level with man's. But He did not change the natural orientation of one sex to the other. Since each one completes the other's personality, woman needs man to help her be a woman and likewise man needs woman to help him be a man. A man or a woman apart from the

other is a human being, but only the two together
constitute mankind.

The Bible does not give meaning to masculinity
and femininity as such. It is through the reciprocal
relationship of these two elements that their purposes
in God's plans are realized. God assigned neither to
man, the male bearer of His image, nor to woman,
the female part of that image, the exclusive responsibility for accomplishing His purposes. Sexual differences are not to be ignored, since each sex derives
its meaning from its distinctive qualities. The dignity
of either sex stems from the divinely ordained correlation of the male and the female destined for
partnership. That dignity resides in each individual's
purpose for being and is the birthright of all, quite
apart from the marriage relationship.[24]

It must be remembered that complementarity is involved in every dimension of human existence, in the
mental and spiritual as well as the physical. Even
in the life and activities of the unmarried, the
principle of partnership must operate. Fulfilling
male-female relationships are possible for them as
together they participate in common tasks.

Further clarification of male-female complementarity might be made by comparing masculine and
feminine kinds of awareness to spotlight and floodlight lighting. The spotlight, in its pinpoint focus,
would represent the male's sensitivity; the floodlight,
in its diffused quality, would represent the female

kind of sensitivity, The floodlight knowing is a
diffused awareness of a whole variety of things going on simultaneously, an awareness that relates the
parts to the total setting. It has been variously
designated as the preconscious, the unconscious, or
the superconscious. It is more commonly referred to
as an intuitive kind of knowing. By contrast, the
spotlight sensitivity is a conscious noticing of
specific aspects of the whole, as details detached from
the total setting. Man tends to focus on certain areas
of experience, while woman sees detail as part of a
wider context.[25] In this connection, psychologist
David C. McClelland of Harvard says that men are
often deaf, dumb, and blind to what is happening in
interpersonal relationships because they are so busy
concentrating on a task.[26]

It is clear that no one would depend exclusively
on either the floodlight or the spotlight for effective
lighting; certain combining of the two is necessary.
The same is true in mankind's awareness of his world.
To the degree that the spotlight knowing concen-
trates on illuminating specific areas and comprehend-
ing them, it ignores what lies outside its focus. The
spotlight kind of attention must definitely be sup-
ported by the diffused floodlight knowledge that keeps
the spotlight on target. The two types of intelligence
need to be recognized for the specific dimension each
brings to a clear understanding of the total situation.
Creative productivity calls for a strong grasp of the

isolated elements while gaining perspective from the general areas of awareness. These two areas of strength must be properly related to each other to prevent a one-sided orientation toward life.[27]

The complementarity of man and woman indicates how independent they are. Both sexes need to understand the important and unique contribution which woman's point of view adds to man's. When her wisdom is combined with man's in every human endeavor, a more perceptive judgment is brought to bear on the issues involved. Such mutuality and cooperation are necessary in all human deliberations, including those of the church. Interdependence is built into the human state because God created His human being in the dual form of male and female. Consequently any self-sufficiency on the part of either sex will result in insufficiency.[28]

New freedoms for woman are making possible a greater degree of personal interrelationships and social cooperation between the sexes. This is leading to a fuller realization of the meaning and responsibilities of their relationship. Further removal of sex disqualification will increasingly enable women to play an invaluable part in the life of the community.

The changing status of woman is resulting in new patterns of interaction between husband and wife. Their worlds are no longer divided into two separate and distinct spheres. As more and more they share one world, the points at which they can genuinely contribute to each other are multiplied. This broadening of complementarity into a variety of experiences brings the potential of fuller and more meaningful marriage relationships.[29] Such enrichment could be equally true of all the broader male-female relationships, for both the married and the single.

Men and women must learn to work together on the basis of their equality as individuals, while capitalizing on their complementary differences. It is known that men tend to concentrate on studying and analyzing a problem; women, on the other hand, tend to focus on doing what needs to be done for the good of the people involved. If it is necessary to bring these two approaches together in the functioning life of the home, should it be considered any less necessary for the best functioning of life in the church or any other part of the social structure?

It is contrary to the best interests of any society for either sex to exercise such power as men have traditionally enjoyed, for it inhibits the creative insights and energy meant to emerge from sexual polarity. When woman is excluded from any effective participation in the councils of men, her complementary feminine genius is lost in decision-making. Many sociologists and other observers are wondering whether this kind of situation might not at least partially explain the recurring crises continually threatening mankind.[30]

Male-female complementarity exists because God,

seeing that it was not good for a human being to live in solitude, created mankind as a dual being. Sex differentiation orients the two parts toward each other in order that they might relate one to the other and become more themselves because of each other. Since this purpose is built into sex differentiation, it can be accomplished only as there is mutuality of relationships between the two sexes in all spheres of living.

Need for Self-Identity

Knowing who she is as a woman is a prerequisite to woman's understanding of her role. She must discover who she is in relation to man, since her destiny is united with his. She must realize the distinctive characteristics of her femininity as compared with those of man's masculinity. But man must likewise know who he is in relation to woman and understand the essence of his masculinity, if the two are to find meaning in their correlation as male and female. The strength of their life together depends on the understanding the two sexes have of their respective identities.

The personal significance of manhood or womanhood is not found in the simple awareness of being male or female evident in biological structure. It cannot be discerned in isolation, but rather is evoked by a genuine personal encounter with the complementary sex. In such a relationship each person becomes aware of a new dimension of experience, that of confronting another human being who is also human, but with a significant difference. Through that experience is perceived something of the deeper and more subtle meaning of sexual bipolarity. Further insight concerning the significance of masculinity and femininity develops according to the quality of man-woman relationships experienced.[31]

Recognizing the differences brought together by man and woman in their relationships can prevent competition since this opens the possibility for effectively combining the assets of both. Awareness of differences in makeup and thinking helps them understand differences in attitudes and reactions that might drive them apart. It also leads them to appreciate and accept each other for what they are, and to be more cooperative in their roles. Each sex should feel a sense of worth in having its own specialties of excellence to bring to the other.

The contemporary male will need to reconceive his notion of masculinity before he can give woman her proper place in his scheme of things. He must learn that he does not need to prove himself superior to woman or to show himself lacking in graciousness to be truly masculine. Many of the traditional qualities attributed to maleness are only characteristics assigned to man as part of a cultural pattern. Mere symbols of maleness should not be confused with genuine maleness.

When man sees his responsibility as a man to help woman rise to her full height as a person, then the two can work together to enrich each other. The male who has no reason to doubt his masculinity will have the capacity to make a woman aware of the full range of her femininity. Likewise a woman who has an unshakable self-awareness of her quality as a woman enriches the maleness of man. And so it is a loss to man when woman fails to realize her full identity, or to woman when man fails to realize his.

Woman, too, must have her own identity to feel sure of her secure place in the scheme of things. She must have respect for herself if she is to feel at peace with herself and with others. Self-acceptance is thus vitally important to her in fulfilling her partner relationship with man. Today's women sense that they have an obligation to develop themselves as persons because they have greater expectations for themselves than simply to fill their limited traditional role. They realize, too, that within the family setting they must determine who they are besides their husband's wife or their children's mother.

Understanding of the self leads to clearer understanding of roles. Since each self is either a masculine or a feminine one, self-awareness also unfolds the functions of each person's masculinity or femininity. Logically, then, a person's role should grow out of the self, but a self recognized as possessing its own

special qualities. Role is not a function to be attached to personhood, but rather is part of its
essential being.[32]

Man and woman venturing forth side by side in
mutual trust will learn through such an experience
how God has destined them to function together. The
fact that mankind was created as a sexual duality
indicates that man and woman as separate persons
have been given no completely fixed or clearly
defined roles. Rather they have been called to be
partners in all of life. But to live creatively in this
partnership, they must be ready to renounce what
is simply traditional, as opposed to what is really
biblical, in their views of each other.[33] Then they
can comprehend that an enriching relationship is the
God-ordained purpose of masculinity and femininity.

Man and woman can successfully discover their roles
when both become more themselves because of each
other. Proper male-female relationships exist only
insofar as the essential being of each partner is
fully respected and allowed to complete the other's
being. When their respective roles are thus determined, each part of the human duality finds its true
place in relation to the other part. When men and
women really can be what each is designed by God
to be, then competition between the sexes will give
way to harmonious and creative cooperation between
them.[34]

With this identity, a truer concept of masculine

and feminine roles can evolve, for these roles can then be viewed more in terms of the qualities each person brings to the relationship than in the delineation of their tasks.

Inadequate Theology of Sex

The confusion in the church as well as in society about the role of woman calls for a close look at the traditional Christian view of man-woman relationships. It is necessary to examine whether its underlying presuppositions are borne out in biblical teaching. Since culturally determined patterns have often been reflected in the church's thinking about male-female relationships and functions, it is imperative that the prevailing negative attitudes toward woman in the church be examined and evaluated.

A study of woman's role as portrayed in the Bible indicates that the factual accuracy of the church's ideas and the soundness of its doctrine on this whole matter might be in question. Furthermore, an obligation rests on the church to communicate to a highly confused society the true biblical concept of God's purposes in the bisexuality of man's creaturehood. Society's perverted attitudes regarding sex are destroying the sanctity of the marriage relationship and promulgating false ideals for fulfillment in man-woman relationships.[35] It is time for the church to bring wholeness into this area of brokenness on the contemporary scene.

The fundamental interdependence of the two sexes and their reciprocal functions means that any unsatisfactory adjustments between man and woman may bring serious personal and social consequences. Inadequate theology concerning this interdependence and reciprocity of the sexes can contribute to such lack of adjustment. A false idea of sex has given society the wrong idea of the true nature of love between a man and a woman. Physical love has become for many the substance and end of love, with the result that the broader base of personal commitment and deep personal relationships is neither considered nor explored. This provides wrong expectations for marriage, which can only prove to be false and deceptive. There is in this view no recognition of the Christian idea that love's primary motive is giving rather than getting. Here a Christian view of male-female relationships should speak to the basic fact in the Christian ethic that the cost of love is sacrifice, which involves the personal giving of oneself to another. This concept must certainly be part of the church's theology of sex.

The church can provide a sound basis for its thinking on this matter only when it recognizes the primary importance of relationships inherent in the bisexual nature of humanity. This must then be seen as applying to human relationships in all areas of life. It would show marriage to be a relationship between two persons who enhance and complete each other as they correlate their respective functions and responsibilities.

Such a premise would give validity to the role of the unmarried woman. It would allow her as a person the freedom of encounter and interchange with men in the world of thought and action. When motherhood is considered woman's chief reason for being -- instead of recognizing that as man's helper her worth lies in her relationships with him -- woman in any other role is regarded as somehow not being within her legitimate role. Consequently the unmarried and the professional women, and at times even the widows, are made to feel left out of things. These persons should be given their rightful place in the church instead of being placed, as it were, on the level of stepchildren.

This view would mean better functioning and more health in the body of Christ, where each member's gifts are needed for the good of the whole body. It would mean that woman, along with man, would be allowed to grow into more maturity in Christ through participation in the discerning processes of the body.

The church, in its theology of sex, needs to recognize that in every relationship on every level there is necessary a certain kind of confidence and faith for success in the relationship. It is the confidence that one is being told the whole truth and that one's opinions are being given due consideration in the deliberations affecting their common life. Forceful domination and the distrust it brings are always destructive of relationships.[36] Woman's faith and confidence in church leadership cannot be destroyed without loss to the body of Christ.

Christ brought into the thinking of the religious leaders of His day a changed order of values regarding woman and her role in His kingdom. The church must find from the Gospels what this new concept was; this is the only way to determine God's eternal norms for the place of woman in His church. The church must rediscover Christ's evaluation of woman as man's equal in the male-female partnership given responsibility for carrying out together God's purposes in the world.

3
Woman's Natural Strengths

Woman is a necessary dimension in the human equation of male and female created in the image of God. The differences that distinguish her as a person from the male are the marks of her femininity. They contribute uniquely to the man-woman relationship.

Many of the special traits associated with masculinity and femininity in a given culture are simply social patterns superimposed upon basic physiological differences. There are, to be sure, some respects in which the natures of men and women are similar. It must also be recognized that there is a great variety in personality patterns and traits within either sex. Hence it is not always easy to distinguish what real differences can be found to exist between the male and the female.

Although the two sexes have been shown to be equal, this does not mean that they are essentially similar or that they can be made so by social conditioning. Anthropologist Margaret Mead says that no known culture has ever expressed articulately that male and female differences are limited to their differing roles in childbearing.[1] Social conditioning does influence the shaping of personality, but research has shown that much of what is considered to be male and female in behavior, personality, and special talents has a biological base.[2]

To identify woman's distinctiveness, it is necessary to discover what in her nature is enduring, what would be true in any society at any point in history. This delineates her real genetic potentiality and her psychological nature as woman. These differences that set her apart from man are not to be found in abilities, other than physical, or in general intelligence. They are rather in her view of things, her interests, and her psychological makeup.

Many of the authorities on social behavior believe that women have a characteristic intellectual style that causes them to see things that men do not see, besides seeing other things differently. They are uniquely and innately equipped to provide certain qualities in the human equation which the male cannot provide. Woman's own sense of worth is largely derived from this discovery. As she attains equality with man and claims her full share of the contemporary adventure, she will do so most fruitfully by remaining true to her psychological nature.

Creator and Fosterer of Life

The most significant difference distinguishing woman from man in every society is woman's role in bearing children. Femininity is basically a woman's orientation to this distinctive quality of bearing and nurturing the human race. With this function she is committed psychologically and ethically to foster life. She has the disposition for this commitment, whether it is realized in motherhood or not.[3] This is the key that unlocks the qualities of her true nature as woman. Her reactions to these essentially female capabilities give her the distinctive psychological characteristics affecting what she does, how she thinks, and how she feels.[4] She is made to be the creator and fosterer of life; she is committed to this no matter how much man may mechanize and destroy life.

Certain traits of character spring from her psychological commitment to the nurturing and preserving of life. She gives herself to the purposeful activity of one capable of maintaining life. She is interested in making environments where people will feel secure. Not only does she concentrate on persons rather than things, but she also seeks to build relationships with them. She is concerned about the feelings of others in interaction with them.[5] The quality of living matters to her.

Woman's special sensitivities and understanding equip her for loving. To give herself in some loving gesture is her greatest source of satisfaction. In a hostile world she is tenderly responsive to all kinds of human need, giving support while attempting to understand. Willing service, complete devotedness, and self-surrender are marks of true femininity.

Almost every woman feels a deep need to make herself completely available to another being, in the kind of relationship so essential to the mother-child relationship. This is part of woman's disposition to preserve life; the very existence of the infant depends upon the mother's ability to reach beyond her own feelings, thought patterns, and physical needs according to the demands of the moment.[6] Herein is found her particular ability to understand the feelings of others and to identify with them in their varying situations.

Her Intuitive Knowing

The various aspects of the feminine mind are closely identified with organic life and its perpetuation. It is from this focus that woman's psychological nature emanates. Woman as knower draws deeply from her function as nurturer. This basic function serves not only as the starting point for her knowing, but also the source of certain qualities characterizing her style of knowing. Thus her social wisdom is closely bound to her psychological nature as creator and fosterer of life.[7]

Woman's knowing is not knowledge completely different from man's; it is rather seeing the facts in a different light. It involves her capacity to possess the special insights of feminine wisdom. These insights are part of a woman's innate intelligence, by contrast to a developed intelligence; they equip her to be sensitive to the needs of those depending on her for their very lives. Such sensitivity is the subtle form of thinking known as intuition. Margaret Mead has concluded from her extensive research in anthropology that intuition is one of the special gifts of woman that makes her way of knowing different from man's.[8]

Intuition is a real faculty possessed by most women in a highly developed form. It is the ability to pick up the nuances and slight details which give a woman signals suggesting an appropriate course of action. The male, who rarely notices the existence of such nuances, feels that women must have some kind of sixth sense. Women are, as it were, always extending their antennae, picking up vibrations of shortwave lengths at the moment they are generated. They can therefore comprehend quickly and act immediately in a given situation.[9]

Women can read the meaning of slight nuances because they are profoundly aware of the feelings of others and are able to identify with their mental state. Helene Deutsch, a distinguished psychiatrist, says that woman's intuition, her understanding of other people's minds, results from an unconscious process by which another person's subjective experience is made one's own through association and is therefore immediately understood.[10]

Since this is a biologically rooted kind of knowing, it is characteristic of woman regardless of whether or not she has become a mother. Always in a state of responsiveness to others and sensitive to their needs, she will be aware of what is happening to persons in a given situation. Bringing such awareness of the human factor into the affairs of mankind at all levels of influence could have a steadying influence upon a tottering society preoccupied with things.

Woman's intuitive approach to life is more apt to be occupied with immediate personal experience, with feelings and longings, and with personal encounters than is man's. His concern is more often occupied with the theoretical, structured knowledge necessary for success in his world.[11] Woman's approach to religious faith is related to her informal kind of knowing. For her it is more of an unconscious urge of the heart, a perceiving, an awareness that moves the will; for man it is more a matter of logical anaylsis and conscious self-discipline. She experiences it as the substance of life grasped in its totality more than as a system built up of separate doctrines.[12]

Woman's intuitive understanding of the human element within a total, complex situation develops competence in dealing with interpersonal relationships. Her social wisdom is important in bringing about constructive change in human behavior. Know-

ing how mutually helpful one person can be to
another, she seeks to build human interdependence
through strengthened relationships. She is therefore
genuinely concerned in understanding the needs and
motives of others. Because she cares about people,
she is attentive to what is happening to them in
interrelationships. She senses where behavior adjustments must be made. Using her subtle intelligence and rapid perception of detail, she can effect
change by gentle persuasion rather than by aggressive
domineering.

Woman sharpens her competence in social understanding when she raises a family of varying ages,
sexes, and abilities. In the complex interdependence
of her world she learns how to get people to cooperate, all the while respecting the individuality of
each one. Women are more expert in deciding how
persons will react to a given situation than men are,
according to research findings.[13] Thus woman has
unique abilities and insights for getting people to
work together creatively. She relies on vision and
skill rather than force to reach this goal. Her
strength lies in interpersonal understandings, not on
competition for power and prestige.[14]

It would seem that these qualities and understandings of woman are much needed in all areas of
human endeavor. They are especially important in
the policy-making and planning aspects of life together in the body of Christ. Woman's insights must

be incorporated into the church's vision of its mission.

Other Related Traits

Other characteristics grow out of woman's fundamental disposition to bear and preserve human life. Her special kind of intelligence –– with its finer perception, sharper intuition, and greater sensibility –– and her responsiveness to others' needs are the sources of other distinctively feminine traits.

Women's attitudes are more conservative than men's, and women tend to be more inner-directed and more religious than men, according to research studies.[15] Woman's view of things involves an intimacy of vision and a direct personal approach going straight to the heart of a situation and perceiving it as it is. Women see details as parts of the whole, in a contextual rather than an analytical manner. They see coherence within the total setting for a sure grasp of reality. This is part of their special way of looking at their world and reacting to it.

Woman's generalized sensitivity, her floodlight awareness, generates a certain kind of soul quality in her living. She tends to form her judgments less out of detached consideration of facts than by following what her heart dictates. For her the logic of the heart has greater significance than the logic of the intellect, particularly as she identifies with persons.[16]

Hence woman is naturally inclined toward the spiritual. Since she is more closely attached to the

fundamental problems of life than man, she knows
that the deepest needs of the human being cannot
be satisfied by what is only material. She shows
greater awareness of her need for seeking moral and
spiritual strength beyond herself; she tends to respond more readily to the message of the gospel
than men do.

Psychologists find that it is a feminine characteristic
to be concerned with values and ideals along with
persons, by contrast with the masculine interest in
structure, along with things. While men follow
straight-line life patterns and are pushed by un-
relenting pressures for tangible results, women are
freer from such external pressures. Their success is
measured more by the quality of their lives than in
steps toward specific goals. Even the woman who
follows a career rarely places material achievement as
the greatest satisfaction in that career.[17]

Men, accustomed to achieving something only by
concentrating, are often surprised at the number
of different things women can do well. Women have
found it possible to achieve success in careers along
with homemaking without shutting family and community responsibilities out of their lives. They have
been able to pursue their many interests in their own
work, in the lives of their husbands and children,
and in community activities, alternating most capably
from one to the other. Because they are always able
to see things in context, they sense where they

need to give up one interest for another at any given moment. When women respect themselves and know what they can do well, they seem able to accomplish more than one person's work.[18]

Since woman's life-style includes paying attention to the whole situation, the total context, details are to her significant parts of the whole. It is from the details that she picks up her cues for action; this is how she senses at any moment what is happening to people. Her awareness of important signals to be caught from even the slightest detail in human behavior makes for thoughtfulness, tact, and discretion in dealing with others. If not properly directed, this feminine trait can be diverted from its helpful positive expression to its negative counterparts of meddling in another's private affairs or spreading gossip. Here the influence of the complementary life-style of the male might help her achieve better perspective.

Woman's attention to detail is essential to her destined task of reacting to the differing needs of others, particularly infants. Details immediate in time and space demand her attention. Showing fine discrimination for things she sees, touches, and hears, she can react to them appropriately and compassionately as well as quickly. Although she is easily touched, she recovers rapidly, ready to react again as is necessary.[19]

What is often thought of as emotional instability

in woman is an evidence of her ability to absorb
the strains put on her by the shocks of life. Scheinfeld likens the female's emotional makeup to the
resilient springs of a car. He says that although such
soft springs would be more sensitive to all the
bumps in the road and would give and vibrate more
than the harder, firmer springs (like the male's
emotional makeup), at the same time they would
take the bumps with less strain. [20]

In her continual attention to the quality of life
for others, woman can more easily than man give
too much of herself without withdrawing to nurture
her own selfhood. She needs to have times of
withdrawal from self-giving into self-nurture if she
is to retain her value to others as God's person helping them to find fullness of life. Neglecting her own
growth as a person may be one of woman's greatest
sins, structured as she is to surrender her own concerns in order to be available to others. This
capacity, so essential to her function of preserving
life, can lead to too much diffusion of purpose, the
tendency to be too easily distracted, and the failure to discriminate between the more and the less
important when she lacks the focus of clear purpose.
Her inclination to merge her selfhood in the experiences of those around her can take the negative form
of dependence upon others for defining her self-
identity and her values. [21]

The increasing desire among Christian women to

follow Mary's example of choosing the one thing needed, the better part over and above Martha's concerns, would indicate their recognition of this peculiarly feminine problem. It is reflected in their widespread participation in small Bible-study groups and spiritual retreats for women. This kind of searching after God and discerning of His will in the company of other such seekers has not been provided to her through the traditional patterns of woman's life in today's church. The impulse for such experiences for women, as well as the planning and direction of them, has come through the separate women's groups existing apart from the male-directed mainstream of church life.

Her Invincibility

Women live not only in the present; they see also the coming into being of the future. This is true because through their children they are constructing the future. They are visionaries who believe that the world as it has come to them can be improved, and are consequently unwilling simply to accept things as they are. It is part of their wisdom to discern what can be changed and what cannot. With this kind of realism, women can be the true visionaries of their day, prepared by their biological destiny to influence history.[22]

Women who believe that they can accomplish desirable change can be invincible. When a situation appears hopeless and there seems to be no way out, the leadership of a woman who refuses to be discouraged may get it accomplished. Relying upon her insights, her faith in people, and her ability to establish meaningful relationships, she conquers the difficulties by sheer will and hard work. Such indomitable women are presently emerging as leaders all over the world. Their sensitivity to the needs of people, their educational preparation, their willingness to cooperate, their ability to organize people, and their faith in something greater than themselves make them choose to stand with others to build a better world. When given a chance, women everywhere have the concern and the dedication to "carry on" and "carry out" according to the terms of their vision and their faith.

An apt illustration of woman's special genius to do what God lays upon her heart to do, no matter how impossible it might seem to be, is found in the life of Gladys Aylward. *The Small Woman* by Alan Burgess is the true story of her missionary work in war-ravaged China. It is an amazing record of one who possessed the inner exaltation and dedication and an abiding tenacity of purpose that helped her do the impossible. As a young girl, she traveled alone by train across Siberia to get to the Inn of Eight Happinesses in a remote area of northwest China. Among the people of that lonely outlying region she lived her faith according to "the same what saying in the Bible" in spite of all sorts of obstacles. Armed with only her forthright experience and her inspired intuitions, she led even a learned Mandarin to faith in Christ. Her crowning act of "carrying on" and "carrying out" was her flight from advancing communist forces across the wild and pitiless mountains without money or food for the 100 children she thus led to safety.[23]

Her feminine ways of feeling, knowing, and acting helped her reach into the stream of life of a people very foreign in thought and culture to that of her simple upbringing as a parlormaid in London.

Women such as this who know what they must do can see their worth as persons and act in unconscious self-possession because they are secure in their own identity. They can respect themselves as women and use their special capabilities to full advantage, knowing intuitively how they can accomplish desired ends by establishing meaningful relationships. A description of Alice Henderson in *Christy* summarizes that kind of life-style. She was pictured as one who accepted herself as she was and who accordingly could accept others with their foibles. After pointing out that she did little criticizing of others for their sins even though she never compromised with wrongdoing or wasted emotional energy on fretting, the characterization continues: "The secret of her calm seemed to be that she was not trying to prove anything. She was and that was all.

And her stance toward life seemed to say: God is —— and that is enough.''[24]

The Christian woman must learn that God has given her an inner nature meant to help human beings reach the height of their personhood, to help them become children of God capable of loving and serving one another. Recognizing that these are the potentialities and capacities with which she is endowed will help her realize her highest possibilities.

But she cannot make her unique contribution to the life and service of the church unless she is an active and responsible participant in its total life. It has been women's lot in the past to be passive onlookers in the life of their societies, subject to the decisions and policies formulated by others. Should this be the pattern in the community of believers, where all are to be members one of another?

Her Unique Contribution

The modern era, which is witnessing great triumphs of science and technology, might be called the "masculine age par excellence" in the sense that it has placed high priority on those aspects of human nature peculiarly significant to men. It has concentrated on external achievement, on the creation of structures, and on the separation of man from nature.[25]

There is a widespread feeling on the part of both sexes that in the face of worldwide dilemmas, the neglected psychological counterforce of woman's person-centered concerns must challenge the priority being given to technological progress. Male thinking shows a fondness for what man can make and for what works, whether it helps to build or to destroy. Feminine thought might be more disposed to sacrifice some technological achievements for the sake of preserving mankind. Women as image providers might thus bring a new perspective into society's ethics of success.[26] It is a known fact that in societies which emphasize maternal principles, greater peace and balance exist in their life together.[27]

Modern society is faced with threats to the feeling of continuity with both the past and the future; this produces an unprecedented social anxiety. These root problems of the human situation cannot be solved by any one group or by members of either sex alone. Woman could bring a necessary dimension to men's approach to these problems, since she has an organic relationship to them. This relationship is bound to woman's nurturing function and her special capacity to bridge biology and history. Her intuitive wisdom, closest to those principles governing the psychological and physical nature of humanity, should be helpful in solving society's root problems.[28]

In his message to the world at the end of the Second Vatican Ecumenical Council, Pope Paul addressed himself directly to women when, as he said, they were acquiring in the world an influence and

a power never before achieved. He commented,
"At this moment when the human race is under-
going so deep a transformation, women filled with
the spirit of the gospel can do much to aid mankind.
. . . Our technology runs the risk of becoming in-
human. Reconcile men with life. . . . Hold back the
hand of man who . . . might attempt to destroy
human civilization."

From many directions authorities in various fields
are suggesting that in the present state of affairs
when the world is suffering from too much male
assertiveness, what is needed above all else is a
realization of the importance of interdependence and
social cohesion in all human affairs. This calls for
understanding in human relations, social poise, and
the skill of persuasion, which are precisely the skills
too often lacking in men's relationships with others.
The women, for whom these interests and skills
come naturally, should be having a more important
role at all levels in the formulating of policy.[29]

Woman, who stands for the significance of individual life, will be searching for what gives meaning
and significance to life. While men establish laws
and create philosophical systems, women will question their validity and challenge their authority.[30]
She is the one in the human partnership who could
change into a home for humanity the society which
has become depersonalized by man's techniques. Humanity is paying a high price for a view of life

determined largely by the male, who has been making the final decisions. This masculine view of the world and the church has placed undue emphasis upon achievement and success at the expense of a meaningful life for mankind.

It must be recognized that from God's point of view it is much more important to be concerned about what is happening in the lives of human beings than to be concentrating on man's great achievements in the physical world. In the church there lurks the same danger. The excitement and satisfaction of achievement in programs and structured activity can be diverting attention from the real mission of the church to change lives.[31] It is the quality of life and its expression in meaningful relationships -- the love one for another -- that should be the distinguishing marks of the Christian community. If it is woman's natural concern to make possible a more abundant life, then she should be expressing her views in ways that count in the church.

Woman, by virtue of her essential qualities as woman, must continually serve to remind man in his pride of achievement that he is incomplete unless he transcends himself. She must keep calling the attention of all that even the noblest purposes are compromised when a person's human dignity is destroyed. She must also help society understand that man cannot accomplish the good life without God.

In a materialistic age which has confused its values,

it is important to recognize the unique contribution woman is prepared to make by emphasizing the kind of values so basic to her view of life. As the one destined to foster and preserve life, she cares deeply about the well-being of the people in her world. She senses the deep meaning of Jesus' declaration that a man's life is not to be found in those things which he can see and handle and use for his own aggrandizement. Luke 12:15.

Modern man needs woman to help him restrain his arrogance, his manipulating for power, and his belligerence. Without the counterbalance of woman's emphasis on personal values, man will continue to display these negative dimensions of his aggressive tendencies.[32] With her insights, her intuitive sensitivity to persons, and her ability to adapt herself to the needs of the moment, along with her concern for important detail, she could help the structure of life to be made more responsive to the values of the person.

Women have much to offer when they are given their place beside men in leadership capacities. They have a personal rather than a strictly academic approach in examining issues, for they relate problems to people as over against simply theorizing. Their special kind of knowing leads them to apply their instinctive and intuitive social wisdom to decision-making. This is by contrast with man's greater need for deliberation so clearly visible in his penchant for study committees. Since women tend to measure success more in terms of interrelationships than in position or rank, they are more ready to act decisively than to parry for the sake of individual stance. For example, they are more prepared to be realistic in order to deal with a difficult personal situation, while men are more apt to act without squarely facing the issue, or to stall for time in an attempt to bypass the issue.

Where women have been admitted to the councils of men, men are discovering that the feminine viewpoint definitely adds new dimensions to former all-male views. This is illustrated in the experiences of Princeton male students when women were admitted to their campus. In a television interview a Princeton male student reported that the outstanding benefit of this change was the different perspective the women bring to classroom discussions.

In addition, women bring to their role as leaders a certain faith in people. They have learned to recognize and accept differences among people. They have an instinctive liking for people and a desire to understand them. As they have learned to cooperate with others, they have brought a kind of social order into relationships. And out of the personal quality of their experiences with individual persons, they have achieved faith in people.[33]

It is not possible to think of woman's role in society at large or in the church without taking into account the unique contributions she is prepared to make to her world. This must be done in the context of the complementarity of her role with man's. The basic considerations that it is not good for man to be alone and that woman is meant to be his helper take on new significance when viewed in the light of women's uniqueness in the matter of male-female correlation.

Woman is meant to be an essential part of the human team God placed on the earth and charged with establishing dominion over it. Since the team is made up of two correlative members, it can achieve balance only when the unique qualities of both parts are brought together in coordinated teamwork. Women's and men's thinking and acting must be combined for achieving total perspective in society's concerns and actions. If the half of mankind's nature residing in woman is ignored or repudiated, mankind will not be reflecting the full spiritual image God placed in its two parts.

It would be more helpful in defining woman's role to do so on the basis of the special contributions she brings to the human equation than on the basis of what she does. All efforts to make a clear-cut separation of the various areas of life between the two sexes are meaningless in themselves. In the workaday world there are really no specifically masculine or feminine professions. Both sexes show themselves capable of doing any kind of work necessary to main-

tain and advance the human race.[34] The pattern of
their functions varies greatly in the differing cultures
around the world. Many roles are assigned to one
sex or the other quite apart from sex differentiation.
It is true that woman's basic characteristics will
often direct her to certain functions in society. Because of her special genius for loving, nurturing, and
preserving life, she will often be performing in roles
involving nurture or care of others. But it is also
true that some men can perform just as capably in
these areas. Men, for example, are entering such
fields as nursing, social work, and home decorating;
they have long been prominent in such areas as
clothing design and food preparation.

It is not really so much what work a woman does
as what she brings to it as a woman, that en-
hances her ministry in the world. The same is true
of her ministry in the church.

Unless the feminine perspective is included in the
organizational pattern of life in the body of Christ,
the result is a male-oriented church. The church
exists to represent and to serve both parts of the
dual being made in the image of God. The unique
characteristics of His image placed in the female
part of generic man are a necessary dimension in
the human representation of God. Therefore woman
must be fully integrated and incorporated into the
functioning life of the church if it is to be indeed His
people unitedly working together as His body.

4
Women Functioning Under God

Throughout the history of God's people women have been contributing in important ways to the life of their times. Even in the Old Testament era, when pagan ideas of womanhood gave little value to woman as a contributing element in human affairs, Israelite women functioned under God as a real part of His people. The New Testament record shows them still more fully integrated into the total life and purposes of God's people as Christ's ministry proclaimed their equality with man in God's kingdom.

After the fourth century of the Christian era, when women were excluded from the organized structure of the church's life and service, their Christian commitment could only be expressed in action outside the framework of the church. In more recent times, as the missionary movement enlarged the scope of the church's effort, women proved to be the driving force in that movement.

It is understood by all that woman has always made a unique contribution in the church through bearing children and nurturing them in the Christian faith. A mother's significance in molding her children's lives is not to be overlooked, since her character greatly influences the character of the home and the learning that goes on in it. A Christian mother can witness in her home to a faith that works. Because her children share life's common experiences with her, they catch the witness of the faith by which she lives.

Several examples from biblical history will illustrate this important role of motherhood. Moses' mother so effectively nurtured her son in his earliest years that he chose in his mature years to identify himself with God's people rather than to accept the rank of a Pharaoh. Through love in family relationships, Naomi communicated to her foreign daughter-in-law the love offered within the family of God. Mary, the mother of Jesus, surely had a significant role in her twelve-year-old son's knowledge of the Scriptures. Timothy's mother and grandmother helped him develop a strong faith in God, which equipped him to spread that faith to others.

Motherhood is a holy calling, but widening the scope of woman's role beyond her home does not imply a negation of the responsibilities of that calling. Christian women can be more totally involved in the life of the congregation without neglecting any home responsibilities they may have. A mother's creative participation in the life of the church can be vital in transmitting to her family the meaning of being members together in the body of Christ.

In a highly developed and secularized society, mothers in the home are facing new pressures to be reckoned with in building into their children's living a strong faith in God. They must themselves be developed persons with informed minds if they are to meet the increased horizons being opened to the young. More than ever they need to be knowledgeable in matters of the Christian faith if they are to be able to transmit it with any kind of effectiveness. They must have the opportunity to understand their own theological concepts and develop their own relationships with Christ. Furthermore they should have more practical training in Christian nurture of the young in such a setting. Involvement in the discerning functions of the congregation could provide them with valuable insights in matters of Christian life and practice.

A technological culture also produces a certain restlessness for the woman in the home. So much has been transferred out of the home that it is no longer either a working or an educating unit. Often it appears to be no longer a center for family living. It almost seems that the mainstream of life is bypassing the home. The Christian mother may feel that she needs to be a part of those processes in the world outside the home which are increasingly shaping the lives of her children.[1]

Woman's long-respected function of providing love

and nurture in the home still stands, but the present situation is making increasing demands on the mother who wants to teach reverence for the family and its relationships in the midst of a society experiencing new social freedoms.

In addition to this traditional role, however, the Bible shows women functioning under God's direction in many additional ways, according to their individual gifts and abilities.

In the Old Testament Setting

Although the world through which Old Testament characters moved was a man's world, Bible women played prominent roles in it. There were prophetesses and outstanding leaders used beyond their usual feminine roles to meet special needs in the religious life of the people. Two women, Ruth and Esther, were worthy of Old Testament books describing their particular roles.

Miriam must have been ministering to her people during their years of oppression, for Micah 6:4 mentions her along with her two brothers: ". . . and I sent before thee Moses, Aaron, and Miriam." At the time of their exodus from Egypt, she was designated as a prophetess, one who spoke forth the Word of God. After leading the Hebrew women across the Red Sea, she led them in a song of exultation over their deliverance at God's hand.

Deborah served Israel well in various capacities;

she was prophet, judge, warrior, and ruler. She attained public dignity and supreme authority such as few women in history have known. Towering above the men of her day, she exhibited a kind of leadership that made her reign stand out as a bright spot in her people's history. She was the keeper of a new spiritual vision that inspired all Israel to trust God.

Esther had the courage of faith and the devotion to her people that prompted her to risk her life to save them. Because she was a woman, she was able to get a hearing from the king and thus be used by God to spare His people from destruction. She illustrates the extent to which a woman will sacrifice herself to do the impossible once she is convinced that it must be done.

Huldah was a prophetess during the reign of Josiah, when a long-lost document was discovered. It was to her that the king sent several men to hear the Word of the Lord for him and all the people concerning the message of the document. Her suggestions for the drastic changes that needed to be effected immediately were taken seriously and were carried out. This is evidence of the respect she commanded as the mouthpiece of God to them.

There are references to women serving in various aspects of the religious life. Some of the Nazarites who assisted in offering the sacrifice were women.[2] The verse in Psalms that speaks of the Lord's Word being published abroad by a great company uses the feminine form in referring to the persons doing this. Hence the American Standard Version translation of this verse is an accurate one: "The Lord giveth the word; the women that publish the tidings are a great host."[3]

Although this is not an exhaustive list, it serves to illustrate that the women among God's people in those ancient times were far more active socially, politically, and spiritually than the women in the pagan cultures surrounding them. It is remarkable that in such a setting, where women did not normally move among the circles of men, there were that many who stand out as having made a real contribution to the life and thought of God's people.

But according to the prophecies of Joel, David, and Isaiah, the prophetesses and women evangelists of the ages to come would far exceed the women of Old Testament times.

In the New Testament Era

The coming of Jesus brought a revolution in the history of woman. Earlier civilizations had held that she was essentially inferior to man. Woman was thought to personify the carnal, and man the spiritual, elements of mankind. Moral and theological discernments were considered as purely masculine endowments. Sin and corrupting pagan influences had robbed woman of her birthright as one created in the image of God. She had lost the dignity of being a person of worth with the same human rights as man.

Christ proclaimed a gospel of human salvation and relationships in which human differences are not to be the basis for any kind of distinctions in the functioning body of committed believers.

The religions of antiquity, like the cultures of which they were a part, were generally male-centered and male-oriented. Consequently they represented masculinely conceived ideals. They did not recognize woman's worth as a person because she was held as being subservient to the male. Since bearing children was regarded as her reason for being, she was given value as a female sex object rather than as a person of worth in all human relationships.

But Christianity as presented by Jesus is neither male-oriented nor female-oriented; it is person-oriented. Its ideals include those identified with true womanhood. There is great significance in the fact that He tolerated, and even welcomed, women among His followers. The devoted band of women who responded so enthusiastically to His call to follow Him indicates their realization that finally they were being given full citizenship in God's kingdom. They, as well as man, were created in the image of God and were capable of relating to Him and sharing in the life of His people.

It is no wonder that women embraced their new freedom in Christ with joy, and devotedly committed their lives to the spreading of His message. As a result they held important roles in the common responsibilities placed on man and woman alike in the Christian communities throughout the early Christian era.

The woman chosen to be the mother of the Savior of mankind was ready to sacrifice her reputation in order to be used by God to accomplish His eternal purpose of redeeming mankind. For a woman in her setting, she showed deep understanding of God's purposes and faith in His trustworthiness. The words of the Magnificat indicate something of why this particular woman was entrusted with the nurture of God's own Son, for they display her capacities to know, to love, and to praise God.

Another woman who had grasped the significance of God's promise of the coming Redeemer was Anna, the prophetess in the temple. The openness of her mind toward God allowed her to recognize in the infant Jesus the Promised One whose coming she was awaiting. And she was able to welcome Him as the One who would be the Redeemer for herself and all those who looked to Him for their salvation. A remarkable discernment of God was manifested in this woman called of God to speak forth His will and word as a prophetess.

Jesus' personal attitude toward womankind was

not summarized by Him in any formal statement. He rather taught His doctrine of woman in a much more forceful manner than mere words. In a day when the religious leaders thought it disreputable to so much as greet a woman in public -- even if this was a wife or daughter or sister -- Jesus openly conversed with women wherever He encountered them.

Not even the disciples were free from this prevailing attitude based on the idea that woman was essentially a temptress in her relationships with man. Being children of their race and time, they were surprised to find Jesus conversing with the Samaritan woman at the well of Sychar. They simply could not understand why He should be doing this. Not only was she a Samaritan; she was also a woman. But subsequent developments clarified His reasons. She was a person capable of the spiritual discernment that was to cause her to accept and to share the water of life which could satisfy the deepest of all human thirsts.[4] Thus Jesus fearlessly showed His disciples that in God's kingdom men and women were to relate to each other in meaningful personal encounters based on personhood rather than sex. Another such declaration was made by Jesus when He permitted the sinful woman to wash and anoint and kiss His feet and to wipe them with her hair.[5]

Jesus also indicated that woman was just as capable of moral and spiritual understandings as man. His conversation with the Samaritan woman is clear evidence of this. His discussion with Mary and Martha during one of His visits in their home further shows His commendation of women who want to be more informed in matters of faith.[6] He did not reprove Mary for being concerned about growing in mind and spirit instead of simply occupying her hands with woman's traditional homemaking tasks. Neither did He suggest that she lacked the understanding or competence to take part in the discussion. He who must certainly have learned spiritual concepts from His own mother, apparently could not accept the notion that women were not fitted to discuss theology with men. And He commended her for wisely choosing how to use her time on that particular occasion. The fact that some of His most profound recorded discussions were with women rather than with the learned doctors was a clear declaration of His estimate of women.

It was in keeping with the custom of the rabbis for Jesus to have had His twelve disciples travel about the country with Him, all the while being their teacher. But it was an unusual thing for Him to tolerate the presence of women ministering to the needs of His group as they could.[7] His acceptance of these women's services would have been beneath the dignity of any rabbi of that day. This in itself was a public statement of His break with the conventional estimate of women.[8] It is interesting to notice that many of the miracles of healing performed as Jesus went about doing good were requested of Him by women. He was ready to listen to their requests and honor them; they were an accepted part of His following.

Jesus' new estimate of women also negated the belief that they were incompetent to make moral judgments. Both Jewish and Roman law gave little worth to the testimony of a female witness and often refused completely to recognize her as a legal witness. No other philosopher or teacher would have deigned to give the first solemn revelation of himself to a woman, as Jesus did to the Samaritan woman. Unlikely as this woman may have seemed as a witness, she proved to be a most effective one. This whole incident must have given the disciples much to ponder over and reflect upon; it could not have been without significance to them. Another woman became the first witness to the disciples of Jesus' resurrection. But they, perhaps because they were still unable to credit the witness of a woman, were not ready to accept her evidence.[9]

All four Gospels show Jesus giving full equality to men and women in the kingdom He was establishing. He indicated not only that the gospel was to be addressed to both sexes indiscriminately, but also that they shared the common duty of bearing witness to it. Both were equally privileged and responsible in being members of God's people.

Woman had again come into her birthright as a child of God. Throughout His ministry women followers remained responsive to His teachings and devoted to His person. And at His death they were among the last at the cross and the first at the tomb, so great was their devotion.

In the Early Church

After the Ascension the apostles returned to the upper room in Jerusalem to await the promised power. Assembled with this group were women, an accepted part of the early church even at Jerusalem; and all with one accord were continuing together in prayer. Acts 2:1-4 relates how all of them assembled there were filled with the Holy Spirit. During Peter's sermon that followed, he explained that what was happening at Pentecost was a fulfillment of Joel's prophecy that sons and daughters would prophesy when God's Spirit had been poured out upon them. It was taken for granted that the Spirit was granted to women and men alike to give them all the same power to witness.

When Paul was sent out by the early church to carry the gospel to other regions, he found women to be very responsive to his message. In Berea their number was so remarkable that they are mentioned before the men, an order of listing that was not customary in ordinary situations.[10]

Wherever the church went, there were women

sharing in winning others to the faith and helping in their nurture. For the most part, they were simply lay women who assisted the apostles in any way they could according to their abilities. The Book of Acts leaves no doubt; Paul appreciated these women and depended on their help.

One of the significant contributions of the women was their leadership in the house churches that were formed as the young church grew. Among Paul's list of valiant helpers in the work of the Lord appended to the Book of Romans, he names women who were helping in five different church groups meeting in their homes. These house churches were centers of activity which soon became focal points for the spread of the new belief.

Many women opened their homes as such centers for the celebration of the love feasts and the further mutually edifying service in which all the members shared. There was no organization of the group, and the women evidently had considerable part in whatever arrangements were necessary. These house groups are most frequently linked with the names of women, which would indicate that they were guiding forces responsible in some measure for the functioning of the group in their life together.

Their worship services were held in the evening. After the love-feast supper came the instructional part of the meeting. The record would suggest that the service was conducted in quite an unstructured manner with all members participating in it. After someone had initiated the teaching on some theme, all were free to add whatever they were moved to contribute by way of a hymn, an exhortation, a revelation, a speaking in tongues, or an interpretation.[11] Sometimes there was the reading of letters from the church in Jerusalem or from Paul or other evangelists. At other times they could meet and hear such traveling evangelists as Paul or Barnabas, who stopped with the different local groups to share stories of their experiences and insights from their broader vision.

In keeping with the communal nature of the primitive church as described in the first part of Acts, other activities must have been carried on in these house churches. They became the centers for teaching the faith to new believers and for propagating the faith. This included the ministry of shepherding, which meant loving and caring for persons to help them become believers and grow in the knowledge of Christ. This kind of ministry seems to have been carried on by the women through the churches in their homes. The traveling evangelists who visited them occasionally were the preachers. But it was evidently the women who continued the teaching and nurturing functions and the daily ministry of love.[12]

Certain women were delegated to carry out special functions. There were the widows, the deaconesses, and the prophetesses.

The widows elected to minister among the needy became a directive force in the church. They apparently adapted their services to the needs around them, and were free to carry them on under their own direction. In ministering to the needy they were undoubtedly visiting the poor in their homes and seeking out those who were open to the gospel. They were expected to show hospitality, especially to strangers. Since their work was built around the particular needs of each Christian group and the special abilities of the widows, their work varied from one group to another.

The deaconess was first appointed to help serve the communal meal. Later she became responsible for the common supplies, and for distributing food and funds to the needy. Phoebe's ministry in this role seems to have included more than this, however.

Prophesying represents another special function performed by women in apostolic times. Paul speaks of both men and women praying and prophesying in the worship service.[13] Philip's four daughters were prophetesses in the service of the gospel.[14] They might be described as women evangelists, joining in the apostles' ministry of teaching the will and the Word of God. They may have helped their evangelist father in instructing the new believers, particularly the women.[15]

Among the women whose names stand out because of their significance in the life of the early church is

Lydia of Philippi. In an act of devotion to her Lord, she placed her home at the disposal of the missionaries to whom she owed her newfound life in Christ. Her house became the first Christian place of worship in Europe. That church, no doubt under her guiding hand, flourished to the extent that Paul could refer to it as his joy and crown. The Acts account of her contribution to this nucleus of the European church is a real monument to what women can do in building the kingdom of God.

The long list of names at the end of the Book of Romans is a clear portrayal of the way men and women worked together at the evangelization of those among whom they lived. The tone of Paul's greetings to these persons who had worked with him in communicating the gospel indicates a warmth of relationship in their fellowship together in the Lord. Nine of the 26 persons named in this list are women.

At the head of this list are Priscilla and her husband, Aquila, whom Paul calls his helpers in Christ Jesus. Although the two of them labored together, the fact that Priscilla's name often precedes her husband's at a time when this was not at all customary, is evidence that she played the more important role of the two. Historical facts attest to her prominence as a member of a distinguished family in Rome; evidence from the catacombs bears this out.[16] It is thought that she may have been more highly educated than Aquila, who was from a different background. Although Priscilla managed her household and helped her husband in the tentmaking business, she was still able to devote herself to a thorough study of the Bible. With her husband at her side, she instructed the learned Apollos, grounding him in a more perfect knowledge of Christian truth. Since the church assembled in their home, it was a center for those wanting to know more about the new faith.[17] Priscilla and Aquila were capable and willing to become real helpers to Paul in teaching and nurturing many in the way of the Lord.

But Paul indicated further that not only he, but all of the churches as well, were indebted to Priscilla. Scholars of early church history suggest that perhaps she had edited Paul's letters before they were sent out to the churches. It has been established that she was with Paul when his letters of Philippians, Philemon, and Colossians are believed to have been sent out from Rome in revised form. Therefore Priscilla is considered as a probable editor of these letters. She would thereby have been of real service to all the churches; the reading of any such letters was an important part of the house church services.[18]

The other women greeted by Paul must have been leaders, or he would not have singled them out for their labors in the Lord with him. The words used to describe the work of these women, as well as that of Euodias and Syntyche,[19] mean participation in the proclamation of the gospel. In the case of Junia, Paul says that she is of note among the apostles.[20] This makes it quite clear that women in the early church shared in the work of evangelism along with men.[21]

It seems that Paul charged Phoebe with the delivering of his letter to the church at Rome. He warmly commended her to them and said that she had assisted many, including himself. It is to be inferred that as a *diakonos* of the church at Cenchreae she was one of the recognized leaders there.[22] The word *diakonos* is frequently used by Paul in reference to himself and others, in which cases it is translated as *minister* or *deacon*. When there was little formalization of offices in the church, Phoebe was evidently "in the service" of the church along with the men.[23]

The record thus shows that in the primitive church many women were participating in the proclamation of the gospel. Never in the history of the Christian church has woman ever taken such a prominent part in this ministry as in the first centuries of the Christian era.

As the church continued to grow and spread, each community established more or less its own pattern of activity. By the second and third centuries it was felt that more standardized patterns and structures were desirable in order to have a general pattern for the whole church. During the third and fourth centuries this process of organizing the church was accompanied by a gradual decrease of women's responsibility in it. The church fathers placed more and more prohibitions on women's participation in church life. The numerous restrictions imposed upon them in the pronouncements of various councils point out the many ways in which women had been functioning prior to that time. They also indicate why one pagan writer's observation had been: "What women there are among the Christians!"[24]

When the church organization had become all male by the time of Constantine, women had to find new outlets for expressing their Christian concerns and interests. No longer having any effective or challenging ministry within the church structure, they began to found women's cloisters, hospices for pilgrims, schools, and hospitals.[25]

Since that period varying degrees of antifeminism have affected the role of women in the church. When women were considered to be the agents of evil forces in society ascribed to them as witches, there was small chance for them to be thought of in very positive terms. Such attitudes about women continued down to modern times, influencing even religious thinking in colonial America.

In the Missionary Movement

During the first 200 years of Protestant mission effort previous to the organization of women's mission work in 1800, the records make no mention of any kind of participation in this program by women. Missionary organizations were were completely dom-

inated by the men. Women who were interested could
do no more than pray for the work, give encouragement to their husbands, or accompany them to the
annual sermons promoting the work of missions. By
the beginning of the nineteenth century, women could
no longer accept such a limited role. They were interested in what was happening in the world. Their
religious zeal generally exceeded that of men. Young
women were beginning to be educated; so they would
no longer be denied an active role in mission work,
even in a day when it was unthinkable for a female
voice to be heard in the church except in the congregational singing of hymns or psalms, or when gatherings of women were to be nothing more than tea
parties where they engaged in social conversation.[26]

Women with capabilities who were devoted to
Christ and wanted to offer their gifts to the church
found the church unprepared to accept their services.
Florence Nightingale faced just such a problem. In
1852 she wrote to a friend about her experience with
her church. She said: "I would have given her my
head, my hand, my heart. She would not have them.
She told me to go back and do crochet in my mother's drawing room."[27] Her desire to serve others in
the name of Christ, however, had to find expression,
and she struggled with her vision of service until at
length she had established nursing as a worthy pro-
fession through which she and others like her could
minister to human suffering. But she regretted that

this could not be done within the framework of the church and under its blessing. Other women have had similar disappointing experiences with their churches, whose leadership completely disregarded their availability to participate actively in the church's mission.

In the second decade of the 1900s Gladys Aylward, a London parlormaid, found that her call to follow Christ by going to China was not recognized as a valid one by those who could have sent her there. In those days it was thought that the normal pattern for a young woman wanting to express her devotion to her Lord was through regular attendance at worship services of the congregation. But she knew that the insistent urging of the Spirit for her to be obedient to her calling was not to be quieted in this manner. She was certain that God was asking more from her than such a mild response. Because she knew with agonizing clarity that she simply had to go to China, she determined to go there even if it meant getting there on her own resources. And she overcame the most impossible situations to do so. Once there she represented God to the Chinese people through the special situations open to her as a woman, and became one of the most effective and outstanding missionaries of the century, reaching both rich and poor with the gospel in her adopted country.[28]

After women's mission societies were organized by American Protestant women in the early 1800s, foreign missions were their consuming passion for more than a century. The story of this missionary movement is summarized in R. Pierce Beaver's well-documented book entitled, *All Loves Excelling.* These societies were the source for all later organized women's activities in the churches and to some extent in the community.[29]

But women's efforts to do their part in spreading the gospel everywhere were not to move forward without meeting obstacles. Ministers and laymen approved of their activities as long as these activities were limited to collecting funds for mission programs and praying for their success, although at first there had been some question raised about whether it was right for women to meet together for prayer. Soon they were also conceded the right to educate themselves and their children regarding mission programs.[30]

Although it was obvious that women were the most numerous and faithful supporters of the mission cause and that the enterprise vitally needed their money gifts, they had no part in determining program and they had to struggle long and persistently for the opportunity to serve in the mission areas. At times they were even denied the right to lead and speak in their own meetings.[31]

The support of the women at home was strengthened as the role of the missionary wives continued to expand. From the beginning, missionary men were expected to take their wives with them. Christian family life could not be exemplified without the presence of Christian families there, and proper respect for woman could not be taught to pagan peoples unless there were women within the Christian community. Although the wife was considered an indispensable part of the family unit, she got little official recognition. Early missionary lists did not so much as mention her name. The husband was the designated missionary and the wife was only an assistant to him, without status among her male coworkers. Later it became evident that only women could approach women in most pagan societies; at that point the wives were seen to have their special role in the missionary effort. It was exciting for the women at home to see the missionary wives exercising a ministry such as no laywoman or pastor's wife in America could expect to exercise.[32]

For the single woman the goal of missionary service was still more difficult to achieve. For a long time the average churchman thought it neither possible nor proper for a woman to go abroad as a missionary without a husband to make decisions and accept responsibility for her. When unmarried women were allowed to go, it was as a kind of second-class missionary, hedged about with restrictions and allowed to exercise little initiative. They were not granted the right to have their own homes, but were to attach themselves to missionary families who would accept them as part of their households. They were not given full missionary status with particular work for which they were responsible.[33]

In time women not burdened by family responsibilities were needed to supervise the schools being established. Some of the unmarried women appointed as teachers and administrators of the schools had the courage and determination to venture beyond their prescribed role and went into village homes and outlying areas to evangelize. The churches organized as the result of their ministry proved their capacity to serve on an equal basis with men as effective missionaries. Even when such women were serving most effectively abroad, many men in the home churches considered it improper for women to speak of their work in the mixed audiences of a Sunday service. Pulpits and platforms were long closed to them. It was an even slower process for them to gain access to conference assemblies.[34]

The missionary movement provided one of the principal ways by which American churchwomen were given increased opportunity for participation in church life. Women have since made a large contribution to Christian mission and service. In some of the large denominations they have had a decisive influence in developing and promoting missionary activity. Yet it remains a fact that the expanded ministry of women found in mission settings is denied them in the work of the church at home.[35] It is indeed a strange phenomenon when what is considered a valid role for women as part of a mission program is not acceptable in the home churches supporting that program.

But it was only through women's separate missionary societies that American women were able to attain full involvement in world mission. Functioning through their own boards they were able to have a role in determining mission strategy, administration, and policy. If they had been allowed to participate on the general boards, they would not have had to form their own. Women have special contributions that they bring as women to the administration of mission work as indicated by the record of their own governing boards. They tend to be more experimental in policy and strategy and are much more prepared than men to take a risk. They show a particular sensitivity for placing persons with special abilities matching the needs into settings of distinct need. They see with the heart as well as with the mind. They have an intuitive understanding of what is involved in a situation. They are impatient with men's bureaucratic procrastination and unending discussion without action. They have the faith and hope making them ready to take risks. They inject into the deliberations a woman's point of view.[36] Here again can be recognized the necessity of bringing together the two complementary parts of bipolar man in order to achieve the balance of total representation.

As the church has taken the gospel to other countries, it has opened to the women of those countries new freedoms. In Africa and the Far East, the church has pioneered in its democratic practices regarding woman's participation in church life. It has demonstrated a new estimate of woman as a person in societies which grant her few legal rights or social privileges. Without giving undue offense to social custom, the church has made sufficient opportunity for women to grow into responsible participation in church life. In China, Japan, and Manchuria qualified women are serving with the men on the governing boards.[37]

In the Japanese churches women regularly help with the ushering, the collection of the offering, and the serving of the communion emblems. When Japanese women become Christians, they sense that they have become full-fledged persons, and they expect to participate fully in the life of the church. This is in contrast with Buddhism, in which a woman is to be subject first to her father, then to her husband, and finally to her son, so that she is never free to act as a person in her own right. At Tokyo Union Theological Seminary there are many women students in attendance. Japanese Christians sense that there is an urgency in getting the gospel out to the people which requires all the human resources available for the task.[38]

On the mission fields where the younger churches have developed their patterns of church life according to biblical principles of life in Christ, women participate with the kind of freedom found in the first-century church. Sometimes women in these churches have a greater involvement in the real work of the church than is possible for their denominational sisters in the American churches.[39]

The Present Situation

The needs of the present age call for the best possible use of all available resources. The church is beginning to realize that a large part of its human resources has not really been incorporated into its functioning life. In general, the abilities of the women have been overlooked because of traditional attitudes about woman's role in the program of the church.

Although more of the women are being educated and trained in special skills and are becoming responsible leaders in the workaday world, their leadership in the church is largely limited to the work of their separate women's groups. Women today know more, experience more, and think more than they have ever done before. Through their thinking and feeling they could add an important dimension to the total life and thought in the church.

Women's ministries in the church have been largely in the fields of teaching, fellowship, and volunteer services of outreach. They contribute heavily to the teaching ministry of the Sunday school and the summer Bible school. They provide the food for church gatherings, sew for the needy, show hospitality to

the stranger, visit the sick and lonely. They do volunteer services in hospitals and institutions in the
community, invite neighbors into their homes for Bible
study or prayer group experiences, or carry on discussions over a cup of tea. No one would question
the value of such services given most willingly by
the women. But many who are happy to give this
kind of service when it is needed feel that they would
also be prepared to contribute in other important
ways.[40]

Many of the responsibilities women have accepted
in relation to church life have been connected with
its housekeeping and social functions. This is more
true in some denominations than in others. This
situation has tended to make woman think of her
activity in the church as an extension of her home
interests. It would seem rather that the Christian
mother should think of her home as the extension of
her church-oriented faith and witness; she should try
to make the home reflect her religious convictions and
commitments in a way understandable to the family
members and all persons who enter its doors for
shorter periods of time. Women must be careful lest
they clutter their lives with too many minor responsibilities that leave them no time to help the church
achieve its true purpose in the community or the
world.[41]

Although women's abilities to educate and to bring
succor to others have been used in a variety of ways,

their ideas are often not really listened to or taken seriously in ordering the life of the church. Frequently their possible contributions to decision-making and strategy-planning have been ignored simply because women have not been considered part of the discernment processes of the church.

Consequently, the church has not yet made use of even a tithe of the vast reserve of talent and devotion to be found in its female members.[42]

5
Members One of Another

The early church was formed in a setting where Jewish and Greek customs forbade women to appear in public. It was in this setting, where the total structure of life revolved around men and excluded women, that the church proclaimed the complete liberty of the individual before God. The church welcomed into its fellowship on equal terms the Jew and Gentile, the master and slave, men and women.

In the fellowship of the church all were alike. Since God was no respecter of persons, those belonging to His kingdom had to free themselves from the social and religious attitudes that considered the Jew superior to the Greek, the master of greater worth than the slave, and the man distinctly above the woman as a human being. They experienced oneness in Christ, and freely shared a common life.

The Roman writer Tertullian commented about male-female relationships in their shared life, describing their fellowship in these words: "Together they pray, together they prostrate themselves, mutually exhorting, mutually sustaining. Equally they are both found in the church of God."[1]

The church of these believers was the example

of what a truly great church should be. It was a loosely structured group of persons from various backgrounds who met together regularly in homes of the members for worship. They prayed, studied, and fellowshiped together in the freedom of the new life they had found in Christ. They had no inclination for ecclesiastical titles or privileges, and had no concern for power or rank. Their common allegiance to Christ made them try to grow in their faith and to bring others into the fellowship whether male or female.

The outlook and pattern of life of these believers was truly being changed as they sought to express in their relationships the new order Christ represented. They sensed that a part of seeing God's glory was to discern how His revolutionary truths were to be applied within the setting of ordinary living.[2] The fresh quality of their living was evidence that they had indeed become sons and daughters of God.

They were now new creatures in Christ intent on establishing a new community in which their Master's directives were being taken seriously. Each one was a vital member of the body of Christ. It was this concentration on their mission as believers that made them unconscious of the human differences that normally would have been separating them.

The Nature of the Body of Christ

The believer in Christ becomes a member of His body by giving himself to Jesus as Lord of his life.

This act of offering all of one's being to Him forever is a response to what Christ represents to the believer. Such a response takes the individual members out of their separateness and rivalry and makes them part of the corporate body in which all see their individual lives in relation to God's purposes for the body.

Because the members are bound together in a common effort to share the good news of life in Christ, they sense that they are all part of one body involving each member in an important functioning part. This results in a genuine spirit of togetherness and a feeling of solidarity as members one of another. Relating to God and His body brings a sense of destiny and meaning to each believer who identifies himself with that body. It is for this purpose that the church exists.

The church is not simply a collection of worshipers who happen to be gathered together as a body of Christians. It is rather the body of Christ in which all the members are integrated into a unified whole; as such it is an organism rather than an organization.

Since the church is a living organism, each member is necessary for the proper functioning of all the other members. "For the body itself is not made up of only one part, but of many parts. . . . If the whole body were just an eye, how could it hear? And if it were only an ear, how could it smell? As it is, however, God put every different part in the body just

as he wished. There would not be a body if it were
all only one part! As it is, there are many parts, and
one body."[3] No one member or group of members
is complete, but is only part of the diversity which
makes of it a functioning unit. The identity of each
member is thus meaningful only as part of the body,
just as an eye or a hand has no significance apart
from the body.

All the members are therefore needed if the body
is to perform normally. "So then, the eye cannot say
to the hand, 'I don't need you!' Nor can the head
say to the feet, 'Well, I don't need you!' . . . . And
so there is no division in the body, but all its different parts have the same concern for one another. . . .
All of you, then, are Christ's body, and each one is
a part of it."[4] Membership in the body dictates the
interdependence of its parts.

Because Christians are members one of another in
Christ's body, all of them must work together as
an organic whole in the life and witness of the
church. If the church is to make its destined impact
in a community or speak with any kind of authority
to an unbelieving society, it must be actively engag-
ing all members in its mission. Each member, male
and female alike, must be given the opportunity to
enter fully into the life processes and the witness of
the church.[5]

Paul's references to the body of Christ emphasize
several aspects of being members together in the

church. At times his stress is on the unity of the body, at other times on the members' responsibility to one another, and sometimes on the body's growth through what the members supply to one another. Because all members share the same experience in Christ, all will share the responsibility of both giving and taking in the functioning of the body. It is only through such self-giving of one to the others that every member will be able to grow into full maturity in Christ.[6]

The Functioning of the Body

All believers, then, are joined together as Christ's body and are individually members of it. This is a body that belongs to Christ and receives its direction from Him as its head. All members are alike subject to Christ as head, and all have the same access to Him.

The body is made up of the necessary spiritual gifts bestowed upon the various members so that the church becomes capable of doing Christ's work in the world. In other words, Christ so constitutes His body that together they unite the diversity of gifts required for the varied ministries of the church.[7] For effectively carrying out its mission, the church must consequently be making use of all the gifts brought to the body through the individual members.

The New Testament epistles refer to functions which pertain to the church's internal ministry of forming and equipping the body itself, and to its external function of mission beyond itself. Both the internal and the external ministries are shown to be the responsibility of the total church. All members are to minister according to the gifts given to them; this is an obligation which each member owes to the other members and to the world.

God gives to each member a special gift needed for the well-being of all. "There are different abilities to perform service, but the same God gives ability to everyone for all services. Each one is given some proof of the Spirit's presence for the good of all."[8] "Each one of us has been given a special gift, in proportion to what Christ has given."[9] "He did this to prepare all God's people for the work of Christian service, to build up the body of Christ."[10]

Since women are included among the members of Christ's body, they have some of the special gifts given to *each one* to prepare *all* God's people for the church's essential ministries. Unless their gifts are sought out and incorporated into the mainstream of its life and mission, the total body will suffer a loss in growth. "Under his [Christ's] control all the different parts of the body fit together. . . . So when each separate part works as it should, the whole body grows and builds itself up through love."[11]

It is time for the church to realize that it cannot grow into full stature in Christ unless each separate part of the body is allowed to function as it should. If

Christ's body is to minister effectively in the present
situation, it can no longer say to its women members that it has no need of them by ignoring their
possible contributions through full participation in its
life. Christ is, after all, seeking to express Himself
through all the believers; He shows no respect for
male above female in the body where He is alike
the head of each member.

Relationships in the Christian community influence
the freedom of each person helpfully to do his part,
for they delineate the functions of the members.[12] If
these relationships are based on sex rather than personhood, it is impossible to develop wholesome, creative interaction between men and women. The kind
of male-female relationships established within the
fellowship largely determines the responsibilities and
opportunities open to its individual members, particularly when they happen to be women. Again it is
important to note that relationships in the church
cannot be separated from woman's role in its life.

Fellowship means mutual love and responsibility,
full participation of all in the shared life of the family
of God. In the life of the church there are to be no
levels of distinction in honor or superiority. If all
members are to fulfill their God-ordained functions in
the body, they must all carry concern and responsibility for the ordering of the church's life. It is necessary for each one to have the possibility of expressing this responsibility. The development of a

church structure that excludes any individual from sharing responsibility for the common life is a denial of the very nature of the church.[13]

The fellowship of the church should provide a setting where the members learn to know Christ better. It should be a community where honesty and openness characterize relationships, creating a climate of trust and willingness to share insights and experiences related to spiritual growth. By looking to one another for direction, the members of the body are mutually strengthened and built up in the faith they are learning to express more clearly. Through such sharing, the Word takes on new meanings as it is understood in the context of personal living. When each member finds freedom to participate in the fellowship, the body becomes so unified and bound together that fellow members sense a deep need for one another.

It is in this fellowship of believers that each person is enabled to be his individual self and to make his own unique contribution to the total group. This is its function of being a healing, transforming, liberating fellowship through which the various gifts of ministry are released.[14] All members, no matter who they are, must be freed to exercise their gifts to help one another. The body grows as every member puts to use the gift given him. Unity develops out of the diversity as each part of the body functions in relation to all the other parts.

As members one of another the church is meant to be a fellowship not only at worship, but also at work in the common tasks of the church. If women are not considered part of the church when it comes to discerning the will of God for the Christian community or planning the strategy for the church in mission, then the church fails to be a real fellowship. The priesthood of all believers to which the church ascribes in theory includes all believers, women as well as men, and lay members as well as the clergy. If woman is to share in the priesthood function of all believers, she should be exercising increasing functions in the church organization according to her gifts.[15]

The obligations placed upon individual Christians in the New Testament writings outline the task of the body of Christ. These obligations might be categorized into the following functions: reconciliation, ministry of love, discernment, admonition, and transmitting of the faith. These five functions are the responsibility of all who confess the lordship of Christ. This means that the church in its pattern of relationships between members must allow each one to be able to participate in all these functions.[16]

Traditionally the church has given women little or no part in the functions of discernment and admonition; these functions have been reserved almost exclusively for the male leadership. Yet no restrictions were placed on the command for Christians to teach and admonish one another; it was given to all alike.[17] Mutual admonishing within the body is necessary for helping one another achieve the life of discipleship. This implies that each member should be able to give as well as take in the process. Likewise if the body of Christ is expected to discern God's will, this process dare not be the function of only one segment of that body. The feminine kind of knowing should be bringing its special insights into this delicate process.

In the early church the Jewish Christian found it hard to believe that the gift of the Holy Spirit, who would guide the believer into all truth, was for the Gentiles as well as for them. Seemingly it has been even more difficult for a male-oriented church to believe that women share equally with men in the Holy Spirit's guidance, particularly in matters relating to the church. The church has not yet understood that oneness in Christ as male and female has precisely the same significance and application as it has in the case of Jew and Gentile.

Until the pattern of church life shows no distinction between male and female, the church will be operating under a faulty structure. Church life and structure can be judged as sound only when it is possible for the body to listen to the Spirit's direction as He speaks through all the members.[18]

Principles of Biblical Interpretation

In the light of all the biblical teachings about woman's role in the functioning life of God's kingdom already referred to in these pages, it is difficult to understand two particular Scripture passages that introduce a different point of view.

Paul tells the Corinthian Christians that women are to keep silent in the meetings of the church where it is a disgraceful thing for them to speak. 1 Corinthians 14:34, 35. Similarly in his first letter to Timothy he says that women are to learn in silence and are not to teach or have authority over men. 1 Timothy 2:11-15.

In addition, some persons feel that the Corinthians passage referring to headship in the order of creation would indicate something of the same idea as the other two references. 1 Corinthians 11:3-16.

Since God's Word must certainly guide the church in decisions regarding woman's function in its life, these statements must be carefully considered. They must be examined in their context and seen in relation to other scriptural teachings about women. All relevant passages from the Scriptures must be brought to bear upon the problem.

The real difficulty in understanding woman's role in the church has to do with how the Bible is read and interpreted. Certain basic principles must be followed in interpreting the Bible. To interpret the Scriptures requires above all an openness to the essential message of the written words.

Often it is not the Bible which divides Christians,

but rather what they bring to the Bible. Approaching the Scriptures with minds that are already conditioned, they readily hear in the Word of God the echo of their own. One can fail to listen to God because of preoccupation with one's own conclusions.[19] It is important to seek to read out of the words what the writer intended to say instead of following the human inclination to read into them what the reader wants them to say.[20]

To understand and interpret the Scriptures rightly it is necessary to be informed about the specific situation to which the writer was addressing himself. Such a situation, for example, gave rise to Peter's advice to women not to braid their hair.[21] Here he was addressing himself to women in a society in which braiding the hair was the sign of the unchaste. This manner of avoiding the appearance of evil had significance only in that particular setting. Therefore this admonition does not apply to the twentieth-century setting, where it would by no means speak to the point in question.

Likewise Paul, within a specific framework, gave advice about eating meat offered to idols and about refraining from marriage. Or again, Jesus told His disciples to walk staff in hand, and commanded the rich young ruler to sell all his possessions. None of these teachings are considered binding today.

What is important in such cases is to grasp all that the words were meant to communicate at that time.

When words were spoken to specific persons or particular situations, it is the intent of those words that must be interpreted and applied in a different setting, where the application of the specific words might be completely void of meaning. What was written in another world must, therefore, be understood in the light of that setting before its original meaning can be transplanted, perhaps in some different form, into another world.

It is also important to know what was the author's purpose in writing any particular Scripture. This is especially true in the case of the New Testament books. The first letter to the Corinthians, for example, was written by Paul in answer to questions put to him about specific problems troubling the Corinthian church.

The basis for interpreting the Bible is the Bible itself. One passage must be tested against other passages, and should be evaluated in the light of what is the comprehensive and pervasive biblical view. Such a view provides an organized summary of views and statements, attitudes and suppositions undergirding the entire biblical message.[22] A case in point is Paul's advice against marriage. His view that marriage was a hindrance to man's best service to God is not borne out by the comprehensive biblical view of marriage as an honorable estate ordained of God for man's good. Consequently most churches do not practice monasticism and clerical celibacy. An honest searching of the Scriptures will force the seeker to return again and again to the Word, comparing one passage with another.

It is not an honest approach to the Scriptures to select only those portions which support a particular idea representing an individual or group viewpoint, while ignoring other relevant passages. All churches and individuals find it easy to be selective in the Scriptures they consider to be binding upon them today. In their zeal to uphold a special point of view, they fail to recognize the blind spots that keep them from developing a total perspective.

Interpretation based on the biblical understanding of things will find its center in the Christ-reality, from which everything in the Bible emanates. The problem of interpreting what God wants to say through the Bible is not to be solved by finding a particular verse to apply to a particular frame of reference, but rather by allowing one's thinking to be thoroughly influenced by what the Bible reveals Jesus to have been, said, and taught.[23] Since the total biblical message is focused upon Christ, all interpretations of the Scriptures can be judged according to their consistency with His teachings. It is from such a position of christological priority that Mennonite theology interprets the Scriptures.[24]

Application of scriptural passages to contemporary life should never be in conflict with what Jesus lived and taught as recorded in the Gospels. It was from this center that the Anabaptists read and interpreted all the other parts of the Bible. Accepting this as their teaching tradition helped them to permit Jesus Himself to be the leading spokesman for His own movement.[25] With this as their locus of authority, they could more clearly discern what in the established church was essentially Christian as opposed to what was man-made tradition.

These principles of interpretation and application of the Scriptures can be of help in considering the problematic injunctions cited earlier. There must be an openness to hear what God is really saying through His written Word, an understanding of the setting for the passages, a comparison of the isolated passage with the total Bible, and a christological approach to interpretation.

The Problematic Scripture Passages

The treatise on headship in chapter 11 of 1 Corinthians has frequently been considered as restricting woman's participation in the worship services of the congregation. On the contrary, this is one of the places where Paul speaks of women who pray and prophesy in the public assembly. What is mentioned in verse four referring to man is repeated in the following verse with reference to woman. Since the very same words are used in both cases, what is said of man's participation must also be true of woman's.

The acts of praying and prophesying in the public

service would indicate active leadership in group worship. To prophesy, according to various definitions, means to declare the mysteries of God for upbuilding and instruction, or to present and apply the Word of God in a teaching ministry.[26]

In verse five Paul assumes that women will be praying and prophesying in the public assembly. If he had thought it improper for them to do this, he would not have bothered to discuss how they were to appear when doing so. He did not forbid the practice, but rather sanctioned it by setting up regulations for it.[27]

Paul here stated that a woman was not to dishonor her husband by participating in the service without wearing her veil. In that culture the veil symbolized the marriage relationship. If a wife appeared in public unveiled it was considered a disgrace to the husband; it was as if she were dishonoring the marriage relationship. Paul therefore asks the Christian wives not to give the impression of renouncing the marriage relationship by violating this custom of public veiling.[28] This is one of the many times in this letter when Paul shows concern for preserving and expressing the sanctity of the marriage bond in the life of the Christian community.

In verses 11 and 12 the mutual dependence of man and woman in the purpose of God is emphasized. Each one owes his existence to the other and is essential to the other, but both alike owe their existence to God and depend on Him. Neither is more closely related to God than the other, for both alike were created in His image. Therefore both are equally responsible before God to fulfill their destiny as His created beings.

This statement of the interdependence of man and woman in the Lord comes as something of a parenthesis in the headship discussion. Here it not only reinforces the complementarity of the male-female duality as expressed in the Genesis 2:18 statement, but provides in addition a glimpse of the Galatians 3:28 insight concerning the unity of all believers in Christ. Evidently Paul felt that in the circumstances at Corinth what needed emphasis was the fundamental view of headship in order to preserve the proper marriage relationship, while in the Galatian setting what was most needed was emphasis on the equality of all before God as a corrective against legalism.[29] It is obvious, in any case, that this chapter would not have been written if women had not been full-fledged, active participants in the life of the Corinthian church.

Then three chapters later in the same book occurs the statement that women are to keep silent in the churches. 1 Corinthians 14:34, 35. This seems to be a contradiction on the part of Paul. Various **explanations** have been proposed in the attempt to **reconcile** these seemingly contradictory statements.

Some suggest that this directive may have referred

to open meetings at which were present unbelievers who might have misunderstood the freedom of these Christian women in a society where it was considered indecent for a woman to speak in public. The other reference might then have been concerned with a meeting such as the love feast, where only believers were present and where woman's freedom in Christ would not be misconstrued.[30]

Another possible explanation is that these public meetings were held in the synagogue at Corinth, and that the Jews were critical of the Christian women's lack of respect for their synagogue law which excluded woman from participation in the service. Hence if these women were causing a problem, Paul might have been saying that in the synagogue they should have the courtesy to abide by synagogue rules. This would be similar to Paul's submitting to Hebrew law in circumcising Timothy, or to his statement that if his eating meat offended a brother, then he would eat no meat. In other words, if these women were doing harm to the Christian cause by causing offense, they should be silent in church and discuss things with their husbands at home.[31]

It might be more significant, however, to note that these two verses are placed in the context of a discussion concerning speaking in tongues. In such a situation, where the believers spoke as they were moved by the Spirit, there arose the problem of keeping the service orderly. Paul is suggesting some patterns to follow for correcting the problem. It is quite conceivable that women, with their natural vivacity and exuberance, could have contributed seriously to a disorderly service, perhaps with more than one trying to talk at the same time. In the interest of good order, Paul could have requested the women to be silent, just as he could order the male prophet to be silent if his speaking did not edify (v. 30). This would seem to be the possibility most worthy of consideration here.

It is quite clear that Paul did not mean for this statement about woman's silence in the services to be thought of as a general directive, for that would be contradictory to what he gave in the same chapter as instructions concerning the conduct of the assembled body of Christ. These instructions as given in verse 26 are as follows: "When you assemble, each one of you has a hymn, a piece of teaching, a revelation, a tongue, an interpretation."[32]

The idea of *each one,* as expressed in the original, must be taken seriously in considering Paul's ideas about woman's participation in the services. At another point in this Corinthian letter he states this same idea that *each one* is given some spiritual gift to be used for the good of all. 1 Corinthians 12:7.

The passage indicating that woman is not to teach or have authority over men is found in another of Paul's letters. 1 Timothy 2:11-15. Some authorities believe this was addressed to illiterate, repressed women who had only recently emerged from heathendom. As such they would not yet be fitted to teach.[33] Others suggest that here the idea of not teaching is meant to be synonymous with not usurping authority.[34]

The problem when this directive is taken as the norm is again that it runs counter to the record of Paul's general attitude toward the place of women in the church as noted in previously cited references, to say nothing of Jesus' own attitudes and teachings on the matter. It is according to the teachings of both Christ and Paul that when man and woman become new creatures in Christ, they are of equal value in God's sight. The differences which separate them in a pagan society become meaningless in their relationships in the Christian community.

The New Testament record indicates that the new status given woman by Christ was continued in the life of the early church. This is further evidenced in examples of early Christian art, in which women are shown speaking in mixed assemblies.[35] The Book of Acts alone is proof that Paul encouraged women to use their gifts in the witness of the gospel and greatly depended on them for help in his missionary endeavors.

The most comprehensive summary of Paul's philosophy of male-female relationships in the church is found in his Galatians 3:28 statement. The supporting base for this conclusion is outlined in Romans 8:33 to 15:7, where he is concerned with the issue of believers who are not being accepted as equals in the fellowship because of outward differences. Referring specifically to the explosive Jew-Gentile problem then troubling the church, he insists on the basic tenet of the Christian faith that all are one in Christ and are all equally responsible to Him. The same reasoning would likewise support the other two categories in the Galatians statement.[36]

It is strange that Paul's total picture of woman's participation in the life of the church has been so completely overlooked in an uncritical acceptance of two of his isolated statements. Through this kind of selective obedience to the Scriptures, a general theological position concerning male-female relationships in the church has been built upon particular directives that are in conflict with the pervasive biblical view on this matter. As a consequence, the role traditionally given to women in the church would seem to indicate an acceptance of society's view of woman rather than God's view.

When the Scriptures are applied to relationships in the setting of contemporary life, it becomes evident whether or not the church is disclosing the God revealed in His Word. The application of the Bible to life situations must always be in harmony with its essential message, which places ultimate value on any person who has become reconciled to God through Christ. It must always reflect the redemptive and transforming purposes of God revealed in the Bible.[37]

Therefore if the church would rightly interpret and apply any scriptural passage with reference to woman's role in the church, this must be approached from God's perspective of woman as one created in His own image, meant to become a first-class citizen in His kingdom.

Living Responsibly as Members

Membership in the body of Christ is the experience of those who have given themselves to Christ as Lord in response to a personal encounter with Him. An honest face-to-face encounter with a God of holiness and love brings the self-awareness that calls forth the desire to serve Him in an act of complete devotion and commitment.

Giving is an expression of self-commitment. What is important in the giver's mind is the heart-given impulse behind the act of giving. Since love is not an abstract thing, it needs to be demonstrated in a tangible expression. Complete commitment, the unreserved gift of one person to another, is love's highest expression.[38]

It is in just this way that the believer finds it possible to express his love for God. In fact, the call to the Christian is to love the Lord with all his heart, soul, mind, and strength. To love someone with this kind of complete self-giving comes most naturally to a woman. When she has laid hold on God and allowed Him to possess her, she can be capable of sincere and courageous devotion.

The Christian woman realizes that it is her responsibility to love God with all her being in precisely the same way that man is to love Him. This greatest of all commands for the Christian is equally binding upon men and women. This command has implications for the church in considering woman's role in its life. The church in practice has seemed to say that it is woman's responsibility to concentrate on loving God with the heart, leaving to man the responsibility of loving Him with the mind. Yet men and women are alike responsible for the completeness with which they have used both heart and mind in the functioning life of Christ's body.

In the congregational worship service a woman may truly yield all her powers to God's command as she sings with earnestness this line from a hymn, and then find that in the following days few of her powers are actually being engaged by the church. When a woman gives herself, she likes to carry out her commitment in tangible actions. But in the church, women are seldom stimulated to use their varied gifts apart from exercising them in their separate women's groups. Often it appears that the variety of their gifts is not even recognized in the male-centered processes of church programming.

In effect, the total church program as seen in its various commissions, boards, and planning sessions would usually give the impression that the men are

at the center of the church's life, with women on the
periphery. Men need to take a long look at the situation and analyze their position. They must decide
whether or not they consider the women to be vital
members in the body of Christ. They must judge
whether the church can afford to waste the resources
of the women, which include their special insights
and their intelligence. They must consider whether it
is right to have only half the members of the body
participate in decision-making.

Many women in the churches are discouraged about
the way in which certain biblical references are used
to justify and support traditionally held opinions concerning women's role in the church. This is done
without examining what the whole teaching of the
Scriptures might have to say on the matter. But when
the church lacks men to carry on essential services,
all kinds of services are gladly accepted from women.
Is it not strange that in other situations theological
reasons are immediately raised against such participation by women? It would seem that theological concepts should be applied consistently; such participation by women should be right in principle if it is
right in any situation. Similarly seminary trained
women usually are found serving in mission programs
abroad; rarely is there a place for them in the churches at home. Again why should their service be acceptable in one place but not in another?[39]

Many women want to have a more vital role in

the ordering of church life because they, too, are members of the body and have concerns and interests which they would like to express. They feel that it is part of their Christian stewardship to give their best talent, skills, and vision to the body of which they are members. They also want to be assured that the church gives them full citizenship in God's kingdom on the same basis as Christ accepts them fully as persons.

Many of the older women in the church who have happily accepted the role assigned to them find it difficult to understand the attitude of the younger women. But these younger women regard this as a matter of Christian integrity. They are seriously concerned about the stewardship of their God-given powers, feeling that they should be using such abilities in the church as well as in the larger community of society. They want to use their special strengths for the greatest good, and feel that they are not fulfilling their purpose as members of the body when they are not exercising their gifts in its life.

The church must never cause its women members to lose respect for themselves as responsible co-workers together with God. Women's role in the church should not cause them to underestimate their God-given powers; it should rather help them develop these powers to the full. Accepting their mission as persons who have grasped the meaning and purpose of life, they want to live with a due sense of responsibility, making the best use of their time.[40] Christian women who have conscientiously developed their special gifts feel that they are not responsibly giving their all in the church when they are not free to carry out what they see as responsibilities laid upon them by Christ.

Jesus asks each individual to follow Him in whatever assignment He may ask that person to do. This is asked of women and men alike. Perhaps the members of Christ's body, like Peter, have become too much concerned about what Christ is calling other members to do rather than making certain that they are following what Christ is calling them individually to do.

The biblical record of women functioning under God indicates that in their times they were called of God to serve in varied ways. Should not today's women who hear Christ's call to follow Him be allowed to obey Him rather than to follow the dictates of man? They feel that their highest responsibility should be to Christ Himself, who is the head of His body.

6
Using All Gifts Creatively

The future of the church is definitely related to its ability to enable all its members to contribute to its total life as fully responsible participants. The church must begin to provide the image of woman as a person made in the likeness of God, working together with man to carry out God's purposes. It must put to significant use the gifts offered to the body by its women members. Creative approaches to the key problems facing the church will not be possible as long as women are not included in the ordering of its life.[1]

The complementary relationship of man and woman is needed in church life. Men and women operating separately fail to have the balance brought by the other element; each element provides its own strengths. Women need to be accepted as full partners before their special sensitivities and attitudes can enter into the church's vision of its mission. The church needs the balance which comes from the combined perspectives of men and women. When both are united in their efforts to be the church under the Spirit's direction, the result will be a stronger church.

Jesus gave no pattern for church structure or of-

fices, but He did enunciate the principles governing
responsible membership in the kingdom of God. Any
church organization of officers dare not violate the
essential nature of citizenship in that kingdom as set
forth in the direct teachings of Jesus. The Holy Spirit
was given to guide the body of Christ in this matter
as in others. The Spirit's function of guiding God's
people into all truth did not cease with the apostolic
church, but continues to be operative in today's
church. [2]

Christ's attitudes and teachings about man-woman
relationships express God's original intent to have
man and woman stand side by side, each one helping
the other. The meaning of this for the church becomes clear in Paul's summary that in union with
Christ there is no difference between man and woman. This is the principle of male-female relationships
that should determine the way men and women work
together in carrying out the functions of Christ's
body. Yet the church in practice has seemed to be
saying that even though before God there is neither
male nor female, in the church's life and worship
this is not to be expressed. [3]

Already in the apostolic church it had become clear
that the principle of there being neither Jew nor
Gentile in Christ could not be neutralized by limiting
its application to individual salvation and privilege
before God, while in all other respects nothing was to
be changed. The record shows that Paul did all he

could to apply this principle in actual working relations within each Christian community. A new unity
between Jew and Gentile was to be discerned not
only by the eye of faith, but was necessarily to be
manifested in the social dimensions of the church as
well.[4]

The church today must realize that the principle of
there being neither male nor female in Christ must
be practiced no less precisely in its life and structure.
Since the male-female situation is placed on the same
level as the Jew-Gentile one, the two are obviously
to be implemented in the same way in the social
dimensions of church life. Just as the early Christians were pioneers of a new kind of relationship in
Christ, so must the church today be pioneers in more
truly expressing the unity and equality of all the
members of the body of Christ in its functioning life.

The church must begin to discern that it is not
enough to overcome only such physical and social
differences as race, education, prestige, or wealth in
the realization that all persons are of equal value in
God's sight. It must understand that Christian equality must likewise be extended to women. If the priesthood of all believers includes women as well as men,
why should they need to depend on men in any way
to work out their salvation for them? The personal
conscience of the individual before God is as much
a part of woman's freedom in Christ as it is man's.

Baptism into the church should be considered an

ordination to a ministry in Christ's body. It was accepted as such in the early church, where every believer freely joined with the other members of the
Christian community in the propagation of the gospel. This was also the understanding in the Anabaptist fellowships, in which both men and women
felt called to share in a common task.

In the past, a woman's power in ecclesiastical matters has been largely in the form of influence. She
has often influenced a man's attitudes or decisions,
but this is not responsible power. She can exercise responsible power only as she acts in her own right.
The churches must now consider allowing her to
exercise responsibility, rather than simply wield influence, as a member in the body.

There are many women in the congregations who
are well qualified to serve on church councils or to
be sent as delegates to church conferences or conven-
tions. Such women could also contribute their gifts
to the church through serving on both local and na-
tional church boards and committees. If the potential
of their knowledge and opinions, ideas and insights,
is not put to use in the ordering of church life, this
is certainly not good stewardship of persons given as
gifts for the good of the whole body. Their voices
should be heard more often and more widely in matters that concern all the members.

There is no scriptural reason for withholding such
participation from qualified women. Taking part in

decision-making or serving as a representative of the body is not a matter of exercising authority over men. Neither is this type of ministry a matter of taking leadership away from the men; it is rather allowing women to assume their responsibility along with the men. One might question why this kind of judgment or fear is often the reaction of men in this regard. Does this reflect their idea of functioning in such capacities? Leaders are to be thought of in any functioning capacity as servants and not lords of the church; their function is to minister rather than exercise authority.[5] It follows, then, that the church should be using their best qualified members for fulfilling its mission regardless of whether they are men or women.

Churches in which mixed boards have become a fairly common experience have discovered that the usual fears and objections to such cooperation are unfounded.[6] They have learned that having men and women cooperate in discussion helps to avoid some of the dangers of abstract and impersonal thinking and achieves more vital encounters between practical living and theological discussions.

There are other areas in which women should be encouraged to develop their potentialities for use in the church. There are those who could contribute significantly as educators, musicians, writers, administrators, and even theologians. Is it not important for women to understand the theology of their churches

and to be able to contribute the insights the Spirit
might be giving through them?

There is need for creative thinking in the church
about kinds of feminine ministry that would take into
account woman's special strengths and concerns.
Women themselves might add valuable insights to
such thinking and planning. Many of them in their
women's organizations are providing responsible leadership in seeking to fulfill the church's essential function in the world.

Women are able to serve the church in a way it
particularly needs, which also happens to be a way in
which they are particularly capable of serving. Today
there seem to remain few easy links between the
church and the life of society. Many of the services
formerly relating the church to the larger community
are now performed by the government or by community voluntary organizations. To those outside it, the
church often appears to be a closed group largely
concerned with its own affairs.[7]

Women find it natural to share ideas across the
garden fence or over a cup of tea or in a small group
discussion with several neighbors brought in. They
meet the mothers of their children's school friends
and become acquainted with their teachers. They
thus have in their natural setting the rare opportunities for again relating the church to the local community. Where they are at work in various social service agencies, there they also have the opportunity of

reaching into homes and families.[8]

Why could the church not recognize this kind of ministry as being an essential arm of the congregation in mission? If women were commissioned by the church to be its representatives in such daily encounters, they could feel that they were functioning as members of the body of Christ rather than simply as individual Christians. This would be giving the status of a lay ministry to women's voluntary and professional services, but it would mean much more than recognition of a significant ministry. It would mean that these persons would see themselves called of God to carry out a special part of the church's task in the community as their particular responsibility.

In addition, there ought to be new kinds of ministries for which seminary programs could offer special preparation. Women might be trained for unique types of ministry in a pastoral capacity where they would be part of a team ministry. One such ministry might be patterned after the deaconess in the apostolic church. Creative ministries for meeting a wide variety of untouched needs of contemporary women might be developed.

Such creative ministries could send trained women out to help women in all kinds of situations where they face problems due to their particular situations. They are the aged, the widows, the single women, the divorced women, the mothers without partners. Each of these groups has its special spiritual, socio-

logical, and psychological problems which the male
clergyman is often poorly equipped to understand.[9]
Or seminary women could seek out some of the many
lonely or destitute women who know nothing of a
meaningful existence. They could give a listening ear
to women in poverty situations, in the professional
world, in rest homes, on the streets, in lonely room-
ing houses or hotels, in prisons.

Out of woman's natural concern for people could
be built the special kind of caring ministry that would
help the church win many through being the servant
of many. Some serious thought should be given to
this whole area by those in charge of seminary programs, together with women who might help give
shape to this type of creative ministry.

Today it is becoming more common in some of the
denominations for women to be ordained to serve as
pastors of congregations. They believe that if there
is indeed no difference in Christ between male and
female, then it might well be that some women would
be called to serve in that capacity today just as they
served as prophetesses in earlier times. The Menno-
nites in Holland have been having women pastors
since early in the present century, and they are convinced that women can function well under God in
this capacity. It is to be recognized that when wom-
en serve as pastors they might have their own approach to the ministry which could possibly give to
it a unique form.

The crucial issue presently facing the church on the matter of woman's role is whether or not the church is ready to make full use of the gifts women members bring as resources for enriching its life and strengthening its message. Obviously not all women have the same gifts any more than men do; some of them may now be functioning according to their gifts. But many have gifts that have not yet been discovered or developed. Others have already proved themselves capable of larger responsibilities in the church. All these resources are needed. It is the responsibility of the church to find them and use them for the good of the whole body.

The question of woman's role in the church is not so much a matter of what tasks she assumes as it is a matter of the relationship she experiences as a member in the body of Christ, where she should be functioning as a fully responsible part of that body together with man.

Footnotes

Chapter One
1. Russell C. Prohl, *Woman in the Church* (Grand Rapids, Michigan: William B. Eerdmans Publishing Co., 1957), p. 37.
2. Derrick S. Bailey, *Sexual Relation in Christian Thought* (New York: Harper and Brothers, 1959), p. 271.
3. Ashley Montagu, *The Natural Superiority of Women* (New York: The Macmillan Company, 1962), p. 186.
4. Franz X. Arnold, *Woman and Man, Their Nature and Mission* (London: Nelson, 1963), p. 16.
5. Bailey, *op. cit.*, p. 270.
6. Otto A. Piper, *The Biblical View of Sex and Marriage* (New York: Charles Scribner's Sons, 1960), p. 79.
7. Bailey, *op. cit.*, p. 282.
8. Montagu, *op. cit.*, p. 189.
9. Bailey, *op. cit.*, p. 286.
10. Seward Hiltner, "The Protestant Approach to the Family," *Pastoral Psychology,* 3, 24 (1952), p. 28.
11. H. R. Hays, *The Dangerous Sex: The Myth of Feminine Evil* (New York: G. P. Putnam's Sons, 1964), p. 281.
12. Montagu, *op. cit.*, p. 29.
13. Hays, *op. cit.*, p. 281.
14. Peter Ketter, *Christ and Womankind* (Westminster, Maryland: The Newman Press, 1952), pp. 47-49.
15. Clara Thompson, "Towards a Psychology of Women," *Pastoral Psychology,* 4, 34 (1953), p. 30.
16. Bailey, *op. cit.*, p. 63.
17. Montagu, *op. cit.*, pp. 24-26.
18. Inez M. Cavert, *Women in American Church Life* (New York: Friendship Press, 1951), p. 22.
19. Ketter, *op. cit.*, pp. 64, 65.
20. *Ibid.*, p. 68.
21. Chester W. Quimby, *The Unity of Mankind* (Anderson, Indiana: The Warner Press, 1958), pp. 103, 104.
22. Elizabeth Achtemeier, *The Feminine Crisis in Christian Faith* (Nashville: Abingdon Press, 1965), p. 144.
23. Ketter, *op. cit.*, p. 69.
24. Edwin C. Lewis, *Developing Woman's Potential* (Ames, Iowa: Iowa State University Press, 1968), pp. 3, 4.
25. Reinhold Niebuhr, *The Self and the Dramas of History* (New York: Charles Scribner's Sons, 1955), p. 220.

26. Franz Alexander, "Emotional Maturity," in Simon Doniger (ed.), *The Nature of Man* (New York: Harper and Brothers, 1962), pp. 129, 130.
27. Arnold, *op. cit.*, pp. 24, 25.
28. Bailey, *op. cit.*, p. 18.
29. Roland H. Bainton, "Christianity and Sex," *Pastoral Psychology,* 4, 31 (1953), pp. 22, 23.
30. J. B. Phillips, *New Testament Christianity* (New York: The Macmillan Company, 1956). pp. 33, 34.

Chapter Two

1. Kathleen Bliss, *The Service and Status of Women in the Churches* (London: SCM Press Ltd., 1952), p. 16.
2. Valerie S. Goldstein, "The Human Situation: A Feminine Viewpoint," in Simon Doniger (ed.), *The Nature of Man* (New York: Harper and Brothers, 1962), pp. 156-158.
3. *Ibid.*, pp. 159, 160.
4. Margaret Mead, *Male and Female* (New York: New American Library, 1959), p. 125.
5. Lewis, *op. cit.,* p. 215.
6. Montagu, *op. cit.*, p. 191.
7. Erik H. Erikson, "Inner and Outer Space: Reflections on Womanhood," in Robert Jay Lifton (ed.), *The Woman in America* (Boston: Houghton Mifflin Company, 1956), p. 2.
8. Lewis, *op. cit.*, p. 230.
9. Robert Jay Lifton, "Woman as Knower: Some Psychohistorical Perspectives," in Robert Jay Lifton (ed.), *The Woman in America* (Boston: Houghton Mifflin Company, 1965), p. 42.
10. Margaret Mead and Frances Kaplan, *American Women* (New York: Charles Scribner's Sons, 1965), p. 35.
11. Edna G. Rostow, "Conflict and Accommodation," in Robert Jay Lifton (ed.), *The Woman in America* (Boston: Houghton Mifflin Company, 1965), pp. 220, 221.
12. Achtemeier, *op. cit.,* pp. 35, 36.
13. Bliss, *op. cit.,* pp. 188, 189.
14. Alice S. Rossi, "Equality Between the Sexes: An Immodest Proposal," in Robert Jay Lifton (ed.), *The Woman in America* (Boston: Houghton Mifflin Company, 1965), p. 106.
15. C. K. Barrett, *The First Epistle to the Corinthians* (New York: Harper and Row, Publishers, 1968), p. 249.
16. Ketter, *op. cit.*, p. 68.
17. *Ibid.*, p. 85.
18. Elliot D. Smith, "The Attainment of Maturity," in Simon Doniger (ed.), *The Nature of Man* (New York: Harper and Brothers, 1962), pp. 135.
19. Achtemeier, *op. cit.*, p. 33.
20. Erikson, *op. cit.*, p. 3.
21. Lewis, *op. cit.*, p. 12.
22. Montagu, *op. cit.*, pp. 54-57.
23. Jeanne Richie, "Church, Caste and Women," *The Christian Century,* 87, 3 (1970), pp. 74, 75.
24. Piper, *op. cit.*, pp. 94, 95.
25. Alan Watts, "The Woman in Man," in Farber and Wilson (eds.), *The Potential of Woman* (New York: McGraw-Hill Book Company, Inc., 1963), pp. 80, 81.
26. David C. McClelland, "Wanted: A New Self-Image for Women," in Robert Jay Lifton (ed.), *The Woman in America* (Boston: Houghton Mifflin Company, 1965), p. 177.

27. Watts, *op. cit.*, pp. 80-96.
28. Montagu, *op. cit.*, p. 91.
29. Armin Grams, *The Christian Encounters Changes in Family Life* (St. Louis: Concordia Publishing House, 1968), p. 63.
30. Bailey, *op. cit.*, p. 283.
31. *Ibid.*, p. 282.
32. Piper, *op. cit.*, p. 37.
33. Bailey, *op. cit.*, pp. 284, 285.
34. Ketter, *op. cit.*, pp. 80, 81.
35. Bailey, *op. cit.*, p. 252.
36. Smith, *op. cit.*, p. 135.

Chapter Three
1. Mead, *op. cit.*, pp. 16, 17.
2. Vance Packard, *The Sexual Wilderness: The Contemporary Upheaval in Male-Female Relationships* (New York: David McKay Company, Inc., 1968), pp. 350, 351.
3. Erikson, *op. cit.*, p. 5.
4. Edmund W. Overstreet, "The Biological Make-Up of Woman," in Farber and Wilson (eds.), *The Potential of Woman* (New York: McGraw-Hill Book Company, Inc., 1963), p. 21.
5. McClelland, *op. cit.*, p. 176.
6. Goldstein, *op. cit.*, pp. 31, 32.
7. Lifton, *op. cit.*, pp. 31, 32.
8. Packard, *op. cit.*, pp. 342, 343.
9. Montagu, *op. cit.*, p. 103.
10. Helene Deutsch, *The Psychology of Women* (New York: Grune and Stratton, 1944-45), vol. 1, p. 136.
11. Lifton, *op. cit.*, pp. 30, 31.
12. Ketter, *op. cit.*, p. 69.
13. Packard, *op. cit.*, pp. 341, 342.
14. Elsie T. Culver, *Women in the World of Religion* (Garden City, New York: Doubleday and Company, Inc., 1967), pp. 236-238.
15. Lewis, *op. cit.*, p. 73.
16. Ketter, *op. cit.*, p. 62.
17. Martha Peterson. Quoted from address at 1969 Convention of American Association of University Women.
18. McClelland, *op. cit.*, p. 188.
19. Erikson, *op. cit.*, p. 18.
20. Amram Scheinfeld, *Women and Men* (New York: Harcourt, Brace, 1943), p. 214.
21. Goldstein, *op. cit.*, pp. 164-166.
22. Montagu, *op. cit.*, p. 99.
23. Alan Burgess, *The Small Woman* (New York: E. P. Dutton and Company, Inc., 1957), pp. 255, 256.
24. Catherine Marshall, *Christy* (New York: McGraw-Hill Book Company, 1967), p. 166.
25. Goldstein, *op. cit.*, p. 162.
26. Erikson, *op. cit.*, p. 2.
27. Mead and Kaplan, *op. cit.*, p. 204.
28. Lifton, *op. cit.*, pp. 48, 49.
29. McClelland, *op. cit.*, p. 187.
30. Piper, *op. cit.*, p. 47.

31. Phillips, *op. cit.*, p. 105.
32. Farber and Wilson (eds.) *The Potential of Woman* (New York: McGraw-Hill Book Company, Inc., 1963), p. 287.
33. Anna L. Rose Hawkes, "Developing Community Leaders," in L. C. Muller and O. G. Muller (eds.) *New Horizons for College Women* (Washington, D.C.: Public Affairs Press, 1960), p. 63.
34. Piper, *op. cit.*, p. 91.

Chapter Four
 1. Bliss, *op. cit.*, p. 192.
 2. Numbers 6:2, 13-21.
 3. Psalm 68:11.
 4. John 4:4-42.
 5. Luke 7:37-50.
 6. Luke 10:38-42.
 7. Luke 8:1-3.
 8. Ketter, *op. cit.*, p. 273.
 9. Luke 24:22-24.
10. Acts 17:12.
11. 1 Corinthians 14:26.
12. Culver, *op. cit.*, p. 67.
13. 1 Corinthians 11:4, 5.
14. Acts 21:9.
15. Ketter, *op. cit.*, p. 431.
16. Culver, *op. cit.*, p. 306.
17. Edith Deen, *All of the Women of the Bible* (New York: Harper and Row, 1955), pp. 227-229.
18. Culver, *op. cit.*, pp. 60, 61.
19. Philippians 4:2, 3.
20. Romans 16:7.
21. Jean Danielou, *The Ministry of Women in the Early Church* (London: Faith Press, 1961), p. 8.
22. Ketter, *op. cit.*, p. 435.
23. Prohl, *op. cit.*, p. 70.
24. Culver, *op. cit.*, pp. 68-71.
25. *Ibid.*, pp. 73, 74.
26. R. Pierce Beaver, *All Loves Excelling* (Grand Rapids, Michigan: William B. Eerdmans Publishing Company, 1968), pp. 15-17.
27. Bliss, *op. cit.*, p. 14.
28. Burgess, *op. cit.*, pp. 15-20.
29. Beaver, *op. cit.*, p. 11.
30. *Ibid.*, pp. 24-34.
31. *Ibid.*, p. 47.
32. *Ibid.*, pp. 48-53.
33. *Ibid.*, pp. 60-64.
34. *Ibid.*, pp. 102-105.
35. Culver, *op. cit.*, p. 54.
36. Beaver, *op. cit.*, pp. 200, 201.
37. Bliss, *op. cit.*, pp. 176-178.
38. Reported by Elaine Sommers Rich.

39. Culver, *op. cit.,* p. 54.
40. Inez M. Cavert, "Status of Women in the Local Church," *Pastoral Psychology,* 4, 34 (1953), p. 21.
41. Culver, *op. cit.,* p. 203.
42. Bliss, *op. cit.,* p. 14.

Chapter Five
1. Prohl, *op. cit.,* p. 55.
2. Phillips, *op. cit.,* pp. 34, 35.
3. 1 Corinthians 12:14, 17-20. This passage and other passages marked "TEV" are quoted from *Today's English Version of the New Testament.* Copyright © American Bible Society 1966. Used by permission.
4. 1 Corinthians 12:21, 25, 27, TEV.
5. Phillips, *op. cit.,* pp. 92-94.
6. Harold S. Bender, *These Are My People* (Scottdale, Pennsylvania: Herald Press, 1962), p. 38.
7. Barrett, *op. cit.,* pp. 292, 293.
8. 1 Corinthians 12:6, 7, TEV.
9. Ephesians 4:7, TEV.
10. Ephesians 4:12, TEV.
11. Ephesians 4:16, TEV.
12. Smith, *op. cit.,* pp. 136, 137.
13. Bender, *op. cit.,* pp. 52, 53.
14. Robert A. Raines, *Reshaping the Christian Life* (New York: Harper and Row, 1964), pp. 20, 21.
15. Cavert, "Status of Women in the Local Church," p. 27.
16. Calvin Redekop, *The Church Functions with Purpose* (Scottdale, Pennsylvania: Herald Press, 1967), pp. 9-20.
17. Colossians 3:16.
18. Bender, *op. cit.,* p. 61.
19. Myron S. Augsburger, *Principles of Biblical Interpretation* (Scottdale, Pennsylvania: Herald Press, 1967), p. 16.
20. David Schroeder, *Learning to Know the Bible* (Scottdale, Pennsylvania: Herald Press, 1966), p. 89.
21. 1 Peter 3:3.
22. Krister Stendahl, *The Bible and the Role of Women* (Philadelphia: Fortress Press, 1966), p. 18.
23. Phillips, *op. cit.,* p. 96.
24. Augsburger, *op. cit.,* p. 18.
25. John W. Miller, "The Sermon on the Mount," *Ontario Mennonite Evangel,* 14, 11 (1969), pp. 3, 4.
26. Prohl, *op. cit.,* p. 29.
27. Barrett, *op. cit.,* p. 250.
28. Prohl, *op. cit.,* p. 64.
29. Stendahl, *op. cit.,* p. 35.
30. Prohl, *op. cit.,* p. 34.
31. Culver, *op. cit.,* p. 59.
32. 1 Corinthians 14:26. (Translated by Barrett.)
33. Cavert, *Women in American Church Life,* p. 25.
34. Danielou, *op. cit.,* p. 10.

35. Culver, *op. cit.,* p. 55.
36. *Ibid.,* pp. 60, 61.
37. Augsburger, *op. cit.,* p. 30.
38. Paul Tournier, *The Meaning of Gifts* (Richmond, Virginia: John Knox Press; 1963), pp. 47-55.
39. Bliss, *op. cit.,* p. 198.
40. Ephesians 5:15, 16. (Adapted from Phillips' translation.)

Chapter Six
1. Peggy Way. "The Church and (Ordained) Women," *The Christian Ministry,* 1, 2 (1970), pp. 19, 20.
2. Bender, *op. cit.,* p. 110.
3. Stendahl, *op. cit.,* p. 40.
4. *Ibid.,* pp. 32, 33.
5. Bender, *op. cit.,* p. 109.
6. Cavert, "Status of Women in the Local Church," p. 26.
7. Bliss, *op. cit.,* p. 199.
8. *Ibid.,* p. 201.
9. Way, *op. cit.,* pp. 21, 22.

Bibliography
of Additional Resource Books

Bailey, Albert Edward. *Daily Life in Bible Times*. New York: Charles Scribner's Sons, 1943.

Bouquet, A. C. *Everyday Life in New Testament Times*. New York: Charles Scribner's Sons, 1955.

Brittain, A. *Women of Early Christianity*. Philadelphia: Barrie and Sons, 1907.

Corswant, Willy. *A Dictionary of Life in Bible Times*. New York: Oxford University Press, 1960.

Eckenstein, L. *Women of Early Christianity*. London, 1935.

Finegan, Jack. *Light from the Ancient Past*. Vol. 1. Princeton: Princeton University Press, 1946.

Latourette, Kenneth Scott. *A History of Christianity*. New York: Harper and Brothers, 1953.

————. *History of the Expansion of Christianity*. Vol. 1: *The First Five Centuries*. New York: Harper and Brothers, 1937.

McGiffert, Arthur C. *A History of Christianity in the Apostolic Age*. New York: Charles Scribner's Sons, 1900.

Spence-Jones, H. D. M. *The Early Christians in Rome*. New York: John Lane, 1911.

Starr, Lee Anna. *The Bible Status of Woman*. New York: Fleming H. Revell Co., 1926.

Streeter, Burnett H. *The Primitive Church*. New York: The Macmillan Co., 1929.

Strong, James. *Exhaustive Concordance of the Bible*. New York and Nashville: Abingdon Press, 1953.

DATE DUE

APR 2 7 2000